DON'T BE DENIED

A simple guide to obtaining a mortgage in today's lending environment

JOE ADAMAITIS

Atom Pie

PUBLISHING

Atom Pie
PUBLISHING

Editorial Director: Laurie Peyser
Cover Design and Book Layout: Lisa Vaal

Published by Atom Pie Publishing, LLC. Rye, N.H.
September 2012
The Atom Pie Publishing brandmark
is a trademark of Atom Pie Publishing, LLC.

This book is written as a source of information only. Every loan
is different, and the rules and regulations of each state differ and may
change from time to time; thus, it is important to consult a mortgage
professional or other professional advisor who has specific knowledge of
the facts of your case and of the specific laws that apply where you live.

For information regarding permissions, contact
Atom Pie Publishing at info@atompie.com.

ISBN-10: 0615686133
ISBN-13/EAN-13: 9780615686134
Library of Congress Control Number: 2012916514

Printed in the U.S.A.

✳

To my parents, Joe and Olga Adamaitis, who instilled
the values of love, family, and hard work in our home.
It's those ideals that inspire my stubborn pursuit of
securing fair lending rights for all homebuyers—rights
supported by a balanced and educational process
designed to help all Americans achieve their dreams.

✳

TABLE OF CONTENTS

INTRODUCTION

The New Lending Environment

Whether you are an excited first-time homebuyer or savvy multiple home purchaser, you must recognize that the world of lending has been drastically updated. Never mind what you've heard or done before; quite simply, the rules and regulations have changed—big time. That's why I've authored this easy-to-read guide on: *How to obtain financing in this new age of lending—without pulling your hair out over the countless new procedural changes.*

Looking back, the housing market and lending world had been stable for nearly 100 years. Sure, the century saw its share of traditional housing cycles, yet within the last decade, specifically from 2004 to 2007, the real estate landscape began its dramatic change. In a mere 36 months, the housing and lending markets saw such greed and ignorance that both industries all but collapsed. Just three short years of ignoring standard rules and guidelines brought the housing market to its knees and allowed mortgage underwriting guidelines to go from being nearly non-existent to imposing extreme levels of restriction. The real estate collapse in 2007 continues to this day to bump slowly along to recovery. By all accounts this is a tragedy of monumental proportions, which as we know creates opportunities for politicians and government to leverage their agendas. We will discuss their role later.

For anyone considering the purchase of a home in 2012 (again, no matter a first-timer or seasoned veteran), you must now understand that *no lender will allow a bad loan to become part of its pipeline.* All lenders operate as if the regulators have a target on their backs—as they are also under constant aggression from investors. Both regulators and investors—such as the Consumer Finance Protection Bureau, Fannie Mae, Freddie Mac and various government agencies—are levying excessive fines and penalties. Making matters worse are the aggressive actions by Fannie Mae and Freddie Mac, who are on a rampage to make up losses by forcing lenders to buy back bad loans from as far back as 10 years ago. Reasons for the buy-backs range from the frivolous to actual errors. The gauntlet has been thrown down, and borrowers must be more prepared than ever when considering purchasing a home.

Underwriters, processors and loan officers are under a microscope to enforce today's guidelines or face unemployment, penalties or even legal action. These people are human, just like you and me, and while they may appear cold or overly demanding in their requests, they are only enforcing guidelines that are dictated by the top banks and the two mortgage giants owned by you and me: Fannie Mae and Freddie Mac.

I'll help you understand the basics of how loans are created from inside a lender's world, and why this is so important to you. This is not a difficult process. Through the easy steps outlined in this book, I will show you how to successfully navigate the maze of complex guidelines and requirements.

But first, a short overview of the core players and how each differs in the world of lending. You can't begin house searching if you don't know how the finance industry thinks and works—and more importantly, who the players are.

There are many types of lenders and they all play numerous roles in terms of how they offer mortgages. In some cases, they present themselves to the public under several different umbrellas and structures. They may take the form of your bank on the corner, who also acts as a wholesale distribution network for brokers, or they may offer correspondent lending for independent bankers, smaller banks and more. Many have multiple organizations under their corporate structures, and these sub-brands service different participants within the lending world.

My intent is not to write an all-encompassing, monster book on mortgage lending, but rather to provide a simple, easy-to-read and easy-to-understand guide that is dedicated to borrowers in today's turbulent market place. I believe that when you have completed reading this book, you will have a solid understanding of how to successfully prepare and apply for home loan financing.

UPDATE: July 12, 2012 — Wells Fargo announced it will no longer provide mortgage brokers access to loan programs

This announcement is a direct result of the government's new regulatory rules under the Dodd-Frank Wall Street Reform and Consumer Protection Act of 2010, which indicates that end lenders will be held responsible for the actions of those such as brokers who sell loans to Wells Fargo, yet who Wells Fargo relies upon for new loan business.

This is a critical turning point for mortgage lending as we know it. Once the big banks begin pulling out of the broker business, competition and service will be lost. To provide you with a simple analogy, consider the implications of the government holding Goodyear Tire responsible for an accident related to a tire that had been sold and installed on a customer's car by a third party retailer such as Sam's Club! In this example, Goodyear would have done nothing wrong except provide a solid product—yet because the retailer incorrectly installed the tire, Goodyear would be penalized.

CHAPTER 1

The Players Standing Between You and Your Loan

It is crucial for anyone in today's home buying market—even those considering a refinance—to understand who the players are. Every lender plays a different role and can affect the outcome of your home purchase. As you will discover in this chapter, the big lenders impact every aspect of the market cycle and the loan process.

In order for borrowers to choose the best lenders for their mortgages, they must understand that it's the big players that drive the mortgage market from the top. Everything the top lending players do or say trickles down to the smaller lenders on the street in one form or another. Whether it's setting guidelines or providing multiple channels for funding smaller lenders through warehouse lines, or specialized departments within the big banks, these top players basically control the market.

At the very top of the heap are two entities that have become somewhat household names, now that taxpayers own them—Fannie Mae and Freddie Mac. They were established as quasi-governmental entities to provide liquidity (money) into the mortgage market place. Fannie Mae was established as far back as 1938, during the Great Depression, and Freddie Mac was established in 1970 in order to expand what is called the "Secondary Market."

The Secondary Market consists of a vast number of investors who buy closed mortgages made by small or big banks, independent mortgage bankers, mortgage brokers and credit unions. When you close a loan with a lender—no matter whether ABC mortgage broker, a small regional bank, XYZ mortgage banker or a credit union—an investor always purchases the paper. This investor could be Fannie Mae, Freddie Mac, another large bank like Wells Fargo or Bank of America or another privately owned bank or entity such as EverBank, BB&T, SunTrust or others.

In the mortgage broker's world, your loan will have already been approved by the investor and the funds you get at closing will be from that entity.

The long and the short of it is that Fannie Mae and Freddie Mac were established to buy loans—meaning to provide money to lenders and investors who make loans. Once the big banks or Fannie and Freddie buy the loans, they pool them and sell them as "Mortgage-Backed Securities," or "MBS." This is a topic we will not devote much time to in this book, as they do not directly help you in your mortgage quest. However, their role was, and remains critical to, keeping the mortgage market alive, or liquid.

More than likely, you have heard the names Fannie Mae and Freddie Mac thrown about as the key players who caused the housing market to collapse. As a mortgage banker for 30 years, I am here to tell you that Fannie Mae and Freddie Mac *were not* the main cause of the housing meltdown. Without pulling in too much of the zany world of politics, it is important to note that the players in Washington, DC, do not want to let on that they knew exactly who caused the meltdown. Even worse, many politicians have followed the likes of Massachusetts Congressman Barney Frank, who has chosen to scapegoat lower-tiered pawns such as small lenders and mortgage brokers—thus eliminating the "big boys" from the scrutiny of the government.

No matter where the fingers point, the meltdown happened and its repercussions acutely affect today's borrowers.

The meltdown: Who? Why? How?

My perspective is that everyone within the industry knows exactly how the meltdown occurred. It was not the small players who caused the initial core spiral. The meltdown involved many players, including politicians, bad Realtors, mortgage brokers, lenders, appraisers and title companies.

However, a collapse of this scale could only start in one place… the top.

As a consumer you can decide for yourself, but I suggest that the meltdown began with the same big players we must now rely on for funding and guidelines. However, before we discuss the big players and their roles, I will insert a bit of political history for you history and political types.

In 1999, then-President Bill Clinton repealed the Glass-Steagall Act of 1933, which separated investment and commercial banking activities in the wake of the 1929 stock market crash. By undoing such a longstanding law, Clinton essentially unleashed (or as current Vice President Joe Biden would say, "unchained") the banks, insurance companies and other institutions to participate in all forms of financial sectors and cross over lines of financial instruments. This paved the way for today's iteration of Wall Street—

and the rest, as we now know, is history.

As you can see, the rules are made at the top, just as in any business; and the instructions for what loan programs may be distributed to brokers and smaller lenders to sell to their borrowers are also mandated from the top. The actions of these players in the lending world are the same as at any sales entity. The sale of mortgages can be likened to a clothing company that designs and sells its lines to many different retail entities—such as department stores, boutique shops and large outlets—yet in this example, the clothing company would dictate the types of clothes that may be sold by which entity, and would require its sales representatives to go out and sell the company's products to every type of sales channel available.

Again, the same is and was true in the mortgage lending industry: Representatives from the big guys aggressively called on brokers and small lenders in an effort to entice them to sell their specific sub-prime programs. It was not uncommon to heap tickets to ballgames or limo rides to lavish dinners, concerts and shows upon brokers and lenders who were only following directions from the top and believed they were selling acceptable loan programs.

This is not to say that people didn't take advantage—as we saw what happened in Florida, Nevada and other so-called "beach and sand" areas. Large flipping scams, coordinated by all of the players, occurred in these regions. Despite appearances and in all fairness, the majority of brokers and smaller lenders were doing exactly what the big banks had told them to do. They had no choice but to offer these programs; otherwise they'd be out of business. They either sold a "Liar" or "No-Doc" loan (for example, where a borrower could lie about how much he or she earns and where the monies come from for a down payment) or they watched clients go to the next lender, leaving them with lost business. Those bad apples who exposed the angles on the bogus loan programs were mostly individuals who entered the business back in 2004 and fled in 2007, taking millions of profits with them. Hopefully, authorities will continue to pursue and incarcerate those folks. I applaud the enforcement, but it must be at all levels and not only focused on the bottom-feeders of the mortgage industry food chain.

For now, the true mortgage professionals are back in control—people who have been in it long before the boom and bust and No-Doc loans. However, let's be clear: As in any business, you will always find those who want to skirt the rules and scam and mislead the clients. When you are shopping for a loan, you must talk to at least three lenders in order to compare their professional suggestions on how best to obtain your financing.

The most important suggestion in this book that I can give you is this: Do not be sold a mortgage—be educated instead! Anyone not willing to help you understand the process, or who is too quick to sign you up, most likely depends on sales ability versus experience and knowledge and will run into trouble getting the job done.

Even after all the hoopla, mortgage fraud continues to rise

You will easily spot the fast-talking fraudster, or at the very least, those who have neither the experience nor the skills to organize and make your loan experience successful. Remember, this process is a work in progress. It is no longer that you apply for a loan and wait; today, you are involved to the very end—and while you may hate your loan officer for bugging you every day for yet another document, be happy he or she is doing the work that will get the job done. It's those who do *not* return a phone call or email that you need to worry about.

As we look more closely at the meltdown, we can identify some of the top participants who teamed up with the likes of Countrywide (purchased by Bank of America) and World Savings (purchased by Wachovia, which was then purchased by Wells Fargo), as well as the old standby telemarketers such as Olympia Mortgage and Champion Mortgage. Lehman Brothers, Morgan Stanley and Goldman Sachs were all players at the time and helped fuel the flames for the boom and finally the bust. The "Pay Option ARM," a program that magically offered borrowers four options for their monthly payments, was also peddled by the likes of Washington Mutual and many of the other big boys. Therefore, the idea that the small brokers and lenders caused this massive problem is like saying the local auto dealership in your hometown caused the meltdown of Chrysler.

Back to the players

You and I, as you now know, have become owners of Fannie and Freddie since the government took them over due to mismanagement. However, they, along with HUD (FHA), VA and USDA, are the entities that put the basic guidelines together for all loan products that lenders rely upon. During the boom and bust, certain players at the top (that I spoke of) sidestepped these entities, resulting in a new series of convoluted guidelines. They worked around the standard rules governing credit scores, property types and loan-to-value ratios (known as LTV, which is the amount of the mortgage compared to the sales price) and ignored other regulations on gifts, co-borrowers or co-signers. In other words, these top players created their own, more profitable guidelines, and ignored the guidelines that the mortgage industry had relied upon for decades, and which had never resulted in a housing collapse of this magnitude.

✳

You should now have a sense of who and what Fannie Mae and Freddie Mac are as they relate to the loan process. Following is a chart of how this all works. It starts at the top with Wall Street, which at one time churned many loans into Mortgage-Backed Securities. Today they participate, but on a much reduced level.

MORTGAGE PLAYERS ORGANIZATIONAL CHART

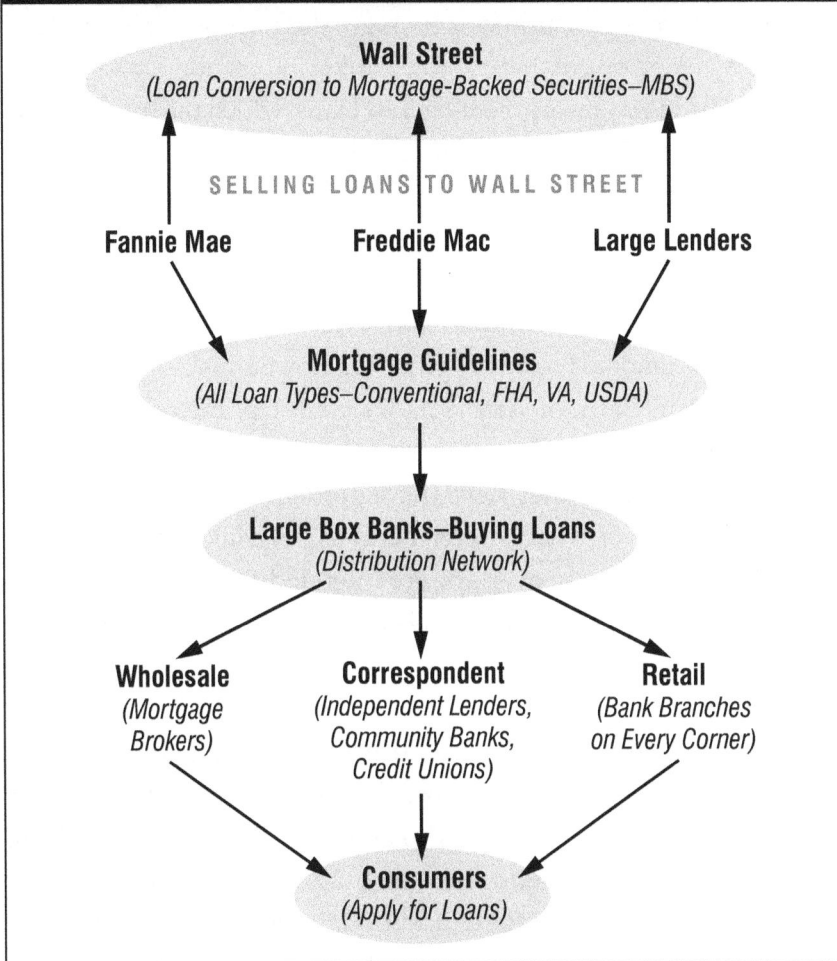

Wall Street
(Loan Conversion to Mortgage-Backed Securities–MBS)

SELLING LOANS TO WALL STREET

Fannie Mae   **Freddie Mac**   **Large Lenders**

Mortgage Guidelines
(All Loan Types–Conventional, FHA, VA, USDA)

Large Box Banks–Buying Loans
(Distribution Network)

Wholesale   **Correspondent**   **Retail**
(Mortgage   *(Independent Lenders,*   *(Bank Branches*
Brokers)   *Community Banks,*   *on Every Corner)*
          Credit Unions)

Consumers
(Apply for Loans)

The important thing to understand is that Fannie Mae and Freddie Mac are the key buyers of loans today. They buy from the big banks, small banks and non-banks (independents and mortgage brokers). Fannie Mae and Freddie Mac, along with FHA, VA and USDA, all make the underwriting rules (as you will read in Chapter 3). Again, these are the same guidelines that were ignored by the folks at top who saw dollar signs in No-Doc/Liar loans and Pay Option ARMs. (I will talk later about how some of these programs were absolutely correct for certain borrowers.)

One important piece of information is to understand that the actual loans for FHA, VA and USDA are not funded by these agencies: They only provide insurance coverage; they do not actually lend mortgage money or purchase loans. Banks and all non-banks simply make and fund the government-backed loans, which the bigger banks buy and then service—which simply means that they collect your monthly payments of principal, interest, taxes, insurance and mortgage insurance (if less than 20% is provided as down payment).

Next in line on the chart, underneath Wall Street, Fannie and Freddie, are those lenders I refer to as the "Big Box Banks"—Chase, Wells Fargo, Citi and Bank of America. They control the market today and get their initial guidelines from Fannie, Freddie, HUD (FHA/ VA) and USDA. Once they have these guidelines, they literally pile more guidelines, or what is referred to as "overlays," on top of the basic guidelines. These overlays are intended to reduce the risk to the lender, as it is the lender who is on the hook if a loan goes bad (as we will discuss later).

The large institutions also provide nearly all the funding to the lenders and brokers who fall below them on the chart. This is what causes confusion to borrowers who go to the FHA or HUD website and read guidelines that do not match up with what their lenders are telling them. Again, these additional overlays are in place to protect the banks from the loan buy-backs we spoke about earlier (by Fannie Mae and Freddie Mac), as well as from borrowers defaulting.

What many consumers don't realize is that the big box gang, who appear to have a branch on every corner in America, also have their hands in nearly every loan made in the US. They do this by using the smaller lenders, brokers and credit unions as "Origination Channels." Most big box banks have other divisions within their corporate structures that are completely focused on earning money from smaller lenders who are out acquiring business under a name other than the name of the big box bank.

Overall, these big players provide nearly 50% to 70% of all loans made in the United States. As an example, Wells Fargo controls 50% of the market with loans it receives from its branches and other channels. These big players simply can't handle all the volume, so they rely on others such as mortgage bankers and brokers to bring in the business. We talk about this next in Chapter 2.

CHAPTER 2

Types of Mortgage Lenders

As we said earlier, the industry is comprised of many different lenders. You will see advertisements on TV from telemarketing types, or ads from a small local mortgage broker or independent mortgage banker. I will explain in detail the differences between the four major types of lenders, which in turn will help you identify the type of lender you want to work with.

From local branches of big box banks to the mortgage company that sponsors your town's youth leagues, you know the names of the various lenders who are involved in helping you attain financing for your home. While their mutual goal is a common one—to secure your loan—how they go about their business, and how the government regulators classify them, can vary greatly. When shopping for a mortgage, you will find yourself with one of the following types of lenders. Use the information to help identify the type of lender you wish to work with.

1. Institutional Banks

Identified as those who are federally insured and take deposits. The list includes the big banks, such as Wells Fargo, Bank of America and Chase, as well as smaller state or regional banks such as BB&T, Regions Bank, Citizens Bank, TD Bank, SunTrust and many other well-known brands. The FDIC or the Office of Thrift Supervision regulates them. Loan officers at institutional banks are registered with the new government entity, the Nationwide Mortgage Licensing System (NMLS*), but are not licensed by each state.

2. Independent Lenders

(commonly referred to as Mortgage Bankers)
Non-depository, and typically but not always privately owned lenders. These lenders include companies such as Academy Mortgage, Prospect Mortgage, REMN and hundreds of others around the country. Loan officers at independent lenders are commonly referred to as mortgage bankers and are registered with the NMLS. They are required to be tested and fingerprinted and must pass an FBI background test given by each state.

NOTE: Every state is different in its requirements, but nearly each one requires that the independent mortgage banker and broker be licensed and tested each year.

3. Credit Unions

Also depositories, but mostly offer limited lending within the traditional standard of Conventional loans requiring a 20% down payment. On occasion, you will find a credit union that may be a bit more aggressive and offer portfolio loans (loans kept in-house and not sold). Loan officers at credit unions are registered with the NMLS and are regulated by the National Credit Union Administration (NCUA).

4. Mortgage Brokers

Typically small, privately owned companies that do not use their own funds to close loans. Brokers (versus direct lenders) rely on numerous lenders to find the best programs and rates to match their borrowers' needs. Congressman Frank and other federal regulators have made mortgage brokers nearly extinct by using them as a scapegoat for the housing collapse. Regulators continue to put pressure on them with new regulations, net worth and reporting requirements. Loan officers in mortgage brokerage firms are registered with the NMLS and are also licensed and tested by each state, the same as independent lenders.

NMLS (Nationwide Mortgage Licensing System): Any consumer can access licensing information about an individual or company operating as a lender in the United States. Simply access this link on the Internet and click on Consumer Access. http://mortgage.nationwidelicensingsystem.org/Pages/default.aspx

As stated earlier, the big box banks, (Chase, Wells Fargo, Citi and Bank of America) all have different channels of business through their various subsidiaries. All banks have "retail" lending, and most have other channels called "wholesale" lending, which provides mortgage monies to mortgage brokers.

Another channel that all of the big banks offer is "correspondent" lending, which is for lenders who fund their own loans. The correspondent channel offers monies to independent lenders who use their own warehouse lines of credit to fund loans, thereby making them direct lenders.

Most banks offer all three channels (subject to the July, 2012 announcement by Wells Fargo) and do this for one important reason: No matter how large Wells Fargo or Bank of America becomes, they cannot get their hands on all of the business and hence, they rely on independents and mortgage brokers to bring them more business with less overhead. However, there is a shift occurring in that thinking, with both Wells Fargo and Bank of America pulling out of the broker business. At the time of this writing, it's a wait-and-see-game where this all ends up.

For the purpose of laying the foundation for you, I will continue under the presumption that other large banks will continue doing broker business—i.e., if you walk into a Wells Fargo branch on Main Street, USA, you will be able to obtain the same loan as if you walked into ABC Mortgage Company or John Jones Mortgage Broker... with your loan ultimately being funded and owned by Wells Fargo.

Ironically, but for good reason, people tell the story that they can obtain a loan faster at the independent's or the broker's office. This is accurate, because the Well Fargo retail branch on Main Street is overwhelmed with clients, while the independent lender or mortgage broker will have a much smaller loan pipeline and be able to offer the fast, personalized service most borrowers seek. The same can be said for mortgage brokers. However, I strongly caution that any attempt to completely rid the industry of mortgage brokers or independents will severely restrict competition and service to the consumer.

To understand how each of these types of lenders works within the mortgage lending environment, Chapter 3 answers the question: "Who makes the rules?"

CHAPTER 3

Who Makes the Rules and Guidelines for Borrowers?

Fannie Mae, Freddie Mac, HUD and USDA are the entities that dictate the guidelines on how any bank, lender, broker or credit union should make a loan and what is required from borrowers.

Fannie Mae:	Federal National Mortgage Association
Freddie Mac:	Federal Home Loan Corporation
HUD:	Department of Housing and Urban Development (provides FHA loans)
VA:	Veterans Administration (provides VA loans)
USDA:	US Department of Agriculture (oversees USDA loans)

The above entities do not create loans, although in 95% of all loan programs in the US, you will find that they have specified the core underwriting rules. However, the large banks overwrite on top of these guidelines in an effort to protect themselves from fraud and borrower defaults; these overwrites again are called overlays, and result in varying required guidelines among banks that hold you, as a borrower, to much stricter standards by the actual lenders. Although the guidelines are in fact fairly standardized, the bigger banks continue to tighten them at this time.

The remaining 5% I speak of is comprised of private investors who also have a piece of the pie with special programs such as those for foreign nationals, or "Jumbo" loans or "Wrap-Around" loans. Private banks or companies certainly play a role in the making of these loans, but a very small one at this time. (Back in the day, they were the movers and shakers of the lending world but they also suffered enormous losses when the collapse began.)

Again, to emphasize why lending is difficult today, if a loan does not meet the guidelines set by the above entities, the organization has the absolute right to deny buying the loan—leaving the lender on the hook for the loan. Lenders are given a short period of time to cure the issues and then must put up the cash to repurchase the loan. Consider that this runs into the billions—with a capital B.

As an example, if John Jones obtains an FHA loan and upon a final quality control audit, the loan does not meet the guidelines, the lender is obligated to repurchase the loan for cash. Once you understand who makes the rules and why your loan must pass scrutiny, you'll understand why your lender is so demanding when requesting all of the necessary documentation.

The next step is to understand where the money comes from. I advise all my clients to treat the loan process as an investigation. As a borrower, you are as close to being on trial as you will ever be. I will say the following again, but I cannot stress it enough:

Loan processors and or loan officers are not mind readers. They have no clue that Uncle Jonnie gave you a graduation gift just before you applied for a loan, or that you sold your car for cash and made a deposit with no notes. Remember, lenders follow every penny—so you must be able to explain circumstances such as where unusual deposit monies came from or why you had four jobs over two years.

CHAPTER 4

Where Does the Money Come From?

Unlike the days of the '70s and early '80s, the money a borrower receives at the closing table today does not come from the deposits of the lender's client (if borrowing from a bank). Back in the 1980s, banks learned a horrible lesson: They felt safe paying 4% to 5% on CDs for their deposit-based customers, and would then make mortgages at 2% to 3% above that number for terms of 15, 20 and 30 years. The banks, back in those days, held onto their loans and did not sell them to Fannie or Freddie—nor did they ever think of securitizing them in bundles to Wall Street.

This worked well for years, until a thing called inflation came along and pushed mortgage rates to 18% to 21% between 1980 and 1981. The banks had to increase the rates they were paying on their CDs, while loan repayments were coming in at low rates of 5% to 6%, setting the banks up for failure. This scenario resulted in the now infamous Savings and Loan Debacle, which put a halt to all lending from deposit-based banks.

So where does the money really come from?

The banks had been seeing the rise of competition from independent mortgage bankers and a few mortgage brokers, particularly in the South, where these entities were much more accepted and recognized early on. The difference was that the independents and brokers did what the banks did not: They opted *not* to fund their loans with their own monies or customer deposits.

Instead, a growing group of investors were buying and packaging loans long before anyone knew the words MBS and "derivatives." These investors would then sell to Fannie Mae as well as to Freddie Mac when they arrived in the early '70s. They went on to increase profits and expand their business by using the MBS and derivative routes to Wall Street. Wall Street had a huge appetite for this paper, and were willing buyers, to say the least.

After inflation hit hard, the banks knew they could no longer use their own monies, and began to eye the practices of the bankers and brokers, realizing they had no choice but to follow their lead and do the same thing—hence the influx of new bankers onto the mortgage scene. The large increase caused an explosion of more investors looking to buy mortgage paper, and the beginning of the securitization of loans to Wall Street.

From here, we'll build on our knowledge and transition to the next chapter, which focuses on the emerging Secondary Mortgage Market.

CHAPTER 5

The Re-Birth of the Secondary Mortgage Market

Lacking capabilities to lend from a deposit base, the banks learned a lesson from the independent mortgage banking companies and mortgage brokers who were closing loans and using monies from other banks and private sources to do so. By using monies from the actual investors, these entities were free from the risk of rising rates. It was a simple concept: Use and adhere to the guidelines provided by certain investors, and pre-sell the loans before they closed. They would make a bunch of money on the sale and go onto the next loan. "No worry-no risk" was the entire concept. The independent mortgage bankers and brokers were onto a concept that the banks recognized as risk-free—that is, until the meltdown of 2007.

Now, with a crisis unfolding against the banks for lending, the Secondary Mortgage Market was in full bloom! This is nothing more than hundreds of entities—both private and institutional, including Wall Street firms such as Lehman Brothers, Goldman Sachs, Morgan Stanley and many others, in addition to Fannie and Freddie—all becoming the new sources of capital for funding loans.

As the years passed and business flourished, Wall Street became embedded to the point that bankers and brokers began creating their own mortgage subsidiaries. Most of these firms were sub-prime lenders and had a strong presence in that arena.

The Secondary Market was now mainstream, and it's where all the funds for closing a loan in today's market come from. However, there is one more piece of information that will help you, the potential borrower, understand how the entire process works: The Secondary Market works differently for each of the types of lenders we described in Chapter 2. Following are two examples:

1. Institutional Banks
These folks take a loan application (known as "originate" or "origination") from the borrower and process the loan using their own monies for closing. Upon closing and funding of the loan, they sell the loan to Fannie Mae, Freddie Mac or even a Wall Street firm. They typically do not sell one loan at a time, but in bundles that can include hundreds or even thousands of loans.

2. Independent Mortgage Bankers
For the most part, these folks originate loans the same way the banks do. Depending on their size and strength, they will sell one loan at a time or under certain circumstances, in bundles to many different investors, including Fannie and Freddie. The independent lender may well be selling to a bank such as Wells Fargo through one of its channels of origination, such as correspondent lending.

Independents typically use their own monies from warehouse lines and therefore are considered "direct lenders." However, the fact that the independent is selling to Wells Fargo—or for that matter, any of the big banks—does not mean that other types of lenders also can sell to Wells Fargo. Brokers did until recently, and today smaller regional banks and credit unions also sell to Wells, Chase, Citi, Bank of America and others.

Obviously, Wall Street and the big lenders have a long reach into every corner of the lending industry. For example, Independent Lender A may sell most of its loans to Wells Fargo using the correspondent channel, while small Mortgage Broker B also sells loans to Wells Fargo, but via its wholesale channel. Wells Fargo then packages loans from both, and resells to larger investors like Fannie Mae, Freddie Mac or Wall Street. Larger independents may also sell to Wall Street, but this is rare.

NOTE: While I continue to refer to Wells Fargo as a wholesale lender, the company's July 2012 announcement about exiting the broker business does not preclude the other big banks from remaining in the business of using and buying loans from mortgage brokers. However, should the trend of exiting the wholesale business continue, the world of lending for borrowers will be one step closer to significantly reduced competition and your lending options limited to only the big banks and independent mortgage bankers.

It is equally important to recognize that all non-banks, which include mortgage brokers and independent mortgage bankers, sell most of their loans directly or indirectly to just four banks: Chase, Wells Fargo, Citi and Bank of America. GMAC (Now known as Ally Bank, and in trouble at the time of this writing) is also a small player but not as large as the others. By "indirectly," we mean that an independent lender or mortgage broker may sell to a small player— such as an EverBank or Flagstar—which then turns around and sells the loan to Wells Fargo.

To understand this better, consider that all the large banks have subsidiaries. While you may see a Wells Fargo branch on every corner, behind the scenes they are also calling on independent lenders and brokers for business. If you remember, Countrywide, along with hundreds of others, sold to these big banks as well as directly to Fannie Mae, Freddie Mac or Wall Street. It all depended on price.

The moral to this story is as follows: All roads lead to the top players. Fannie and Freddie and all the others make the rules. Wall Street and the big banks provide the money (liquidity), and no matter where the borrower applies for a mortgage, the closed loan ultimately will arrive at one of the top four banks, at least 95% of the time. This creates securities for Wall Street and profits that go to the top players The lender may also sell loans directly to Fannie and Freddie, which then turn around and bundle to Wall Street.

As a smart borrower, you must keep your eyes open to news about lending. When news affects the big banks negatively, it trickles down to all players, including independents, regional and community banks, as well as mortgage brokers. They are all linked together, so what happens at the top affects the entire industry, right down to the individual borrower.

CHAPTER 6

Choosing the Right Lender

As part of this overview, we will touch upon the differences between applying for a loan with an Institutional Bank (including a Regional Bank and Community Bank), an Independent Lender (commonly referred to as Mortgage Bankers), a Credit Union and a Mortgage Broker. The exercise in this chapter features a five-phase comparison to help you understand the differences between lenders from a processing perspective. (To gain insight into the differences among lenders regarding service, jump ahead to the grading system outlined in Chapter 21.)

Specifically, each phase is broken out into the following:

- Loan Application
- Processing and Underwriting
- Closing
- Funding
- Servicing

Choosing an Institutional Bank

Banks are broken down into two categories:

1. Large big box banks
   (such as Wells Fargo, JPMorgan Chase, etc.)

2. Regional banks, community banks and credit unions

When a borrower applies at one of the larger banks, he or she can expect that the loan will be taken by either a registered loan officer or a designated financial services representative. The financial services rep's job is to help start the process in the branch, then refer the borrower to a registered loan officer within the bank. Once the loan is passed to the loan officer, it is reviewed and passed onto a processor. The processor organizes the loan documents and when all requested information has been provided, submits the file to the bank's underwriter for approval.

Every step of the process requires review upon review. If any information, documentation or explanations are requested, the borrower is required to provide that information prior to hearing about any approval.

Upon loan approval, the loan is sent to the closing department, which coordinates with the closing agent designated to close the loan. This person may work in an attorney's office or title company, depending on acceptable state laws. (Every state is different as to whether a title company or an attorney's office closes the loan.) Closing agents verify all figures for taxes and insurance purposes, and confirm that all documentation necessary for closing has been properly prepared.

Total estimated time from loan application to closing—in a big bank—could take between 60 and 120 days, depending on local volume. Large banks generally work with centralized processing and underwriting departments, versus local or in-house, so are naturally a borrower's first choice since there is typically a branch on every corner. Borrowers who have made this choice have seen many delays over the past few years and big banks have earned a well-deserved "F" for execution. The delays have a huge impact on borrowers, as contracts expire and deposits can oftentimes be lost.

If you close with a bank or credit union, your monthly statement will usually come from that institution. Most other types of lenders do not service their loans; however, there has been a recent movement by many of the large independents to begin servicing their own loans. You will never see statements from a mortgage brokerage firm, as they are too small.

The definition of servicing a loan is to collect your monthly payment, taxes and insurance.

Recapping an Institutional Bank

Loan Application:	*Taken by a registered loan officer or financial services representative*
Processing and Underwriting:	*Normally out of state in a centralized location*
Closing:	*Handled off-site at a centralized location*
Funding:	*Uses its own monies and bundles large packages of loans to be sold to Fannie and Freddie or securitized by Wall Street*
Servicing:	*The bank where you applied services your loan 99% of the time*

NOTE: At the time of this writing, new bank guidelines being instituted by the Bank for International Settlements (BIS) and a global committee named the Basel Committee on Banking Supervision, which oversees stress testing of all banks worldwide from a capital perspective, are beginning to drive banks away from the loan servicing *business. In the future, borrowers are likely to see private companies providing the servicing. If you're bored on a rainy or snowy night (depending on where you live) and want to read more about Basel and the BIS, go to <u>www.bis.org</u>.*

Choosing a Regional Bank or Community Bank

Every part of the country has regional banks as well as local community banks that provide nearly the same services as the big box banks, but on a much smaller level. These smaller banks use registered loan officers to take the loan application, either in person or online. The process is different from the big banks, as they typically use local processing and underwriting. Statistics show that those who use in-house processing services perform well ahead of those who do not. You need only ask your favorite Realtor for a reference on who performs best in your community.

Smaller banks process and underwrite in the same way as the large institutions, and typically use their own funds for closing. They sell off loans in a variety of ways: Sometimes one at a time, and other times as multiple loans to a variety of investors including Fannie Mae, Freddie Mac and others. Turnaround time is reasonable at 30 to 45 days, depending on the strength of the operation.

<u>Recapping a Regional Bank or Community Bank</u>

Loan Application:	*Taken by a registered loan officer in person or online*
Processing and Underwriting:	*Normally in-house*
Closing:	*Handled in-house*
Funding:	*Uses its own monies and sometimes bundles small packages of loans to a variety of investors*
Servicing:	*Varies*

Choosing a Credit Union

Credit Unions are a completely different animal in that they typically serve a specific client base. For example, there is a Navy Credit Union and a Teachers Credit Union, and employees of companies such as Lockheed Martin have Lockheed Martin Credit Union. The main difference between credit unions and banks is that credit unions are owned by their members. However, many are open to the public and offer the standard plain vanilla loans, as well as an occasional portfolio loan (a loan kept in-house), such as an adjustable rate mortgage.

Most credit unions offer in-house processing and closing, but many rely on outside contractors. They process and close loans like any other lender. Funding, however, can happen in a number of ways; in some cases, such as with a small credit union, funding is similar to independent mortgage companies and mortgage brokers: They use their own funds to close and are reimbursed upon sale of the loan. To the borrower, this is a transparent process. Turnaround time is usually 30 to 45 days, depending on the strength and quality of the in-house team.

<u>Recapping a Credit Union</u>

Loan Application:	*Taken by a loan officer in person or online*
Processing and Underwriting:	*Normally in-house*
Closing:	*Handled in-house*
Funding:	*Uses in-house or warehouse lines, or a variety of investor funds to sell their loans*
Servicing:	*Usually sold to a private firm or large bank*

Choosing an Independent Lender
(Mortgage Banker or Privately Owned Lender)

Independent lenders are privately owned or incorporated companies that do not have the ability to take deposits. These firms specialize in one thing only: home lending, either for purchase or refinance. The loan application is taken by a registered and licensed loan officer in person or online.

Processing and underwriting is a combination of in-house and centralized, depending on the entity. Closing is typically done in-house. Funding of the loan is with the lender's own monies through warehouse lines of credit. Upon closing, the loans are sold to various investors including Fannie Mae, Freddie Mac, Wall Street and a host of others. Turnaround time is usually 30 days or less.

Recapping an Independent Lender

Loan Application:	*Uses a line of credit from one of the larger banks or regional banks, or may choose to use their own funds*
Processing and Underwriting:	*Typically in-house*
Closing:	*Typically in-house*
Funding:	*Uses its own monies and sometimes bundles small packages of loans to a variety of investors*
Servicing:	*Loan is always sold, but this is rapidly changing due to new regulations*

Choosing a Mortgage Broker
(Privately Owned Entity)

Our last group combines the use of all of the above in one form or another. Typically, a mortgage broker operates as a one- to 20-person shop, and may be larger in rare cases. They do not have their own monies, and do not typically use warehouse lines of credit due to costs, administration of the line and risk of being unable to deliver a loan on time. Mortgage brokers are able to shop a borrower's rate among numerous lenders and are usually very competitive. The loan application is taken by a registered and licensed loan officer in person or online.

The difference with mortgage brokers is that they do not typically have their own in-house processor or underwriter, and in fact rely on many different underwriters from many different lenders, depending upon who has the better deal of the day. While this sounds attractive—and with a good broker, it can be—the fact that there are new people (underwriters) to work with every day, versus the familiarity of the same people with the same guidelines, can make the process burdensome for the broker and sometimes, for the borrower. A "good" broker is worth their salt and can be a good choice.

Closing is no different than in any other lending environment; however, funding is completely different compared with nearly all lenders. Funding is solely through the investor, who has agreed to purchase the loan, unless the broker has chosen to use a warehouse line, which is very rare. The negative side to using the investor for funding would be if a last-minute issue arises; direct lenders can be more flexible. Turnaround time is 30 days, but can be longer.

Recapping a Mortgage Broker

Loan Application:	*Taken by a registered and licensed loan officer in person or online*
Processing and Underwriting:	*Underwriting is from a different source for each loan, depending on how many sources the broker uses. The underwriter is not in-house.*
Closing:	*Handled outside*
Funding:	*Uses investor monies for all funding*
Servicing:	*Always sold*

Now that I know the difference, who do I apply to?

Choosing which lender will work best for you is a personal decision. The best person who can point you in the right direction continues to be the same person it always has been for years in this industry... your Realtor! Your Realtor will know which lender gets the job done—and gets it done on time in his or her local market area.

Keep in mind that your Realtor will not know which lender has the best rate. We will discuss rates in Chapter 21. However, I advise you to rely on the experience of your Realtor when seeking the lending option that is best for you, as he or she will be familiar with the banks and independent mortgage bankers or brokers in your area. Call each lending recommendation to discuss your loan options—and take notes! Do this with two to three lenders, rely on what you've read in this book, and trust your instincts.

Understand, without any doubt, that the big banks will not give you the personalized service you want. They may have the lowest rates, but will not deliver in most cases. This has been true for the last several years and common sense confirms the statement:

Big banks rely on volume, and if they are doing 10,000 loans a month, the question you will want to ask is: How will my loan stand out in that pile?

CHAPTER 7

The Home Buying Process

Along with the downward spiraling market came strict new guidelines. The meltdown also brought those who did not get caught in the crisis to the market, with hopes of capitalizing on others' woes. One thing became abruptly and blatantly clear to all participants: This was not your typical cycle or process. Realtors learned quickly to stop wasting time and gas with tire kickers who were not serious or thought they were going to pick up a hot property for practically nothing. There were even those who thought they could qualify but with the new rules in place, they soon found that they never would. A new learning curve was now the norm, not just for buyers and sellers, but for Realtors and mortgage professionals.

If you are in the market, you must be aware of the overall conditions related to lending. Your goal is to watch, listen and learn—from the news releases in your local paper or on TV to diligent research on the Internet.

This chapter lays out the actual process in full. The following chapters will describe each step in even more detail.

Typical home buying steps in today's market

1. Pre-approval – See Chapter 8

2. Begin the process of gathering items listed in the Lender's Checklist

3. Choose the best Realtor – See Chapter 10

4. Provide the Realtor with your pre-approval letter

5. Begin your home search

6. Make an offer on the home

7. Review the contract – know what you are signing!

8. Accept the offer – now what?

9. Apply for a home loan – if you have not yet applied, you must do so immediately

10. Prepare for upfront costs:

    a. Inspection ($375 to $600)

    b. Survey (if required, $375 to $600)

    c. Pest report (if required, $150 to $275)

    d. Appraisal ($325 to $500)

    e. Home- or condo-owner's policy (to be paid in full at market rates, prior to closing)

    f. Home inspection (different than an appraisal) ($350 to $450)

11. Provide any and all documents your loan officer, processor, or underwriter is requesting, immediately! Not the next day or the next night… immediately means now!

12. Schedule the closing – upon approval, the title company or law firm will schedule

13. Prepare to wire the closing funds in advance (instructions will be provided)

14. Attend the closing

Pop the champagne and move in!

CHAPTER 8

Pre-Approval vs. Pre-Qualification

There is a substantial difference between pre-approval and pre-qualification: A pre-approval is a complete review of credit, assets, income and employment, while a pre-qualification is a minor review without verification of a borrower's financial status. A pre-qualification is simply not enough anymore. In years gone by, pre-quals were fine; not anymore!

Before the crisis, lenders would pre-qualify borrowers without checking credit or reviewing pay stubs, W-2s and bank statements. A true pre-approval is when you submit a full loan application (in person or online) and supporting documents. Your credit is pulled, and you must provide W-2s, pay stubs, and bank statements to show you have the income and assets to support your ability to purchase and close. If you are self-employed, the pre-approval requires your tax returns to ensure you are not carrying losses from businesses or income properties.

If you speak with a lender who claims to be able to qualify you, be sure to inform the representative that you are not interested in a simple pre-qualification—which is nothing more than simple financial calculations—but that you need *full pre-approval*!

NOTE: *If your lender only wants to provide a pre-qual, it's time to move on to a savvier lender.*

How does a pre-approval work, and how do you know if you qualify for a mortgage?

One of the greatest myths to lending is that many people believe this is a complex calculation. In actuality, it's about as simple as it gets. To qualify *financially*, a borrower must show three things:

1. Annual monthly income

2. Gross monthly payments for all debts including credit cards, car loans, student loans, etc.

3. Sufficient assets to close the deal

To begin, all loans require that the borrower meet debt-to-income and housing debt-to-income ratios. These are the two key ratios which underwriters review to determine a borrower's stability. The one ratio that really matters is the *total* debt-to-income, which we talk about in Chapter 15.

Let's take the first step to finding a lender for your pre-approval. If you are already working with a Realtor, ask him or her. This first step is where you must apply the research we spoke of earlier. During this time, you may be guided to a lender—which is fine, but now apply what you've read, as you need to know the lender is right for you and can provide the type of service and program you need. Nine times out of 10, the Realtor will know the right person, but you still need to ask the questions:

a. Can they close on time and within a reasonable timeframe?

b. Do they have in-house processing and underwriting?

c. What's their current turn time to close a loan?

d. Are they local or are they sitting a long ways from the community?

If you have not been working with a Realtor, ask family and friends for a referral. Go online and research loan officers in your area. Ask business associates if they know of a reputable person, or call and ask a well-respected real estate firm. You may also reach out to a title company or law firm that does real estate closings, but again, the best bet is the Realtor.

NOTE: The only time I would be cautious is when a real estate firm or even a builder has their own in-house lenders. There continues to be incentives for the agents and the borrowers to use these firms, and sometime the best deal or service is simply not there.

Once you have names and begin calling, I suggest that if you cannot reach the person immediately, or if they do not return calls within an hour, move on. Identify how many years the person has been in lending. If they say five to seven years, be sure they have expedited their knowledge to today's market conditions, as so much has changed. The reason for this is as follows: Thousands of loan officers came into the business from 2003 to 2007. They were not required to be fingerprinted, nor did they need to be cleared by an FBI background check. More importantly, they did not need to know how to put a loan package together due to the craziness of lending during those times.

A No-Doc (or Liar) loan was essentially comprised of a two-page application with no documents required to support income or assets. Hence, you've had loan officers who have never had a clue about how to properly take a solid loan application. Worse, they had no need to understand guidelines, as they were so loose. If you cannot find a seasoned pro, you may be better off today with someone who has two to three years experience, has been trained properly to take a thorough application, understands supporting documentation and has not been tainted over the past several years by working with sub-prime loans.

CHAPTER 9

Hooray, I'm Pre-Approved! Now What?

The best buyers are those who have begun the preparation for the loan process before they've looked for a home. They have spoken to an expert Realtor, been pre-approved and understand what's necessary to pursue financing. The following are steps you can take to help ensure readiness:

1. Create a New Home Mortgage File once you believe you are in the market. Insert all financial documents into your new file: W-2s, pay stubs, tax returns and asset statements.

2. Begin reviewing your bank statements for any deposits that are out of the ordinary, as you will need to supply the lender with an explanation and documentation of where these deposit monies came from.

3. Stop shopping! This means all shopping that requires a credit check, which may drive down your credit score. You will also need to explain every inquiry on your credit report. For example: Don't buy a new car or open new

credit cards.

4. Prepare for substantial cash out-of-pocket to pay for numerous items prior to closing on your loan. To name a few typical costs, you will need cash up-front for insurance, surveys (where applicable), pest reports, inspections and homeowner's insurance policy.

5. Prepare for the total purchase cost. Many borrowers are not prepared when they see the complete costs of buying a home. Besides the down payment, there are the items above that we spoke of—then you have closing costs, which are the most unexpected of all. Closing costs can be as much as 5% of your purchase price and in some cases, much more.

6. Select your expert Realtor, if you have not contacted one along the way. The Realtor will want to know you have spoken to a mortgage lender before showing you any properties.

As you move forward in the loan process, the person processing your loan will have many questions about issues related to employment, income, assets and credit. The processor is not being discriminatory; he or she is simply asking the questions that require answers in advance of submitting your loan to an underwriter. Think of their jobs as private investigators: They need to tie every large deposit, every credit inquiry and/or every employment gap into the loan application so it makes sense to an underwriter. Everything you can do in advance to help the processor understand your specific scenario—such as a letter of explanation addressing anything that is somewhat uncommon—will substantially help in approving your loan.

Consider the following scenarios:

• You are a nurse or doctor working for multiple organizations and your pay stubs are from four different employers, but your W-2s show just one. Write an explanation.

- You have had numerous jobs over the last 24 months. Jot down, in detail, dates of employment along with your job titles and positions, your monthly gross income and phone numbers and addresses for each job. This will help the processor understand who you are and the type of work you did, and whether you are moving up or there was a lateral move.

Anything you can do to explain certain issues, whether job, asset or credit related, will go a long way toward expediting your loan application.

Today's processors are no longer simply paper pushers. They are trained technicians who delve into fraud checks, loan officer licensing, IRS transcripts and much more. As I will keep reminding you, lending has changed dramatically—however, getting a mortgage *is* attainable, and not as difficult as some would lead you to believe. It simply takes understanding, organization and a keen eye for detail to succeed.

CHAPTER 10

Choosing the Best Realtor

The home buying process begins first and foremost with contacting a Realtor. Not just any Realtor: If you are to succeed—and this includes even those who have been down the path of home buying previously—this is not the time to work with agents who are not:

- Reputable

- Extremely knowledgeable about the market

- Able to give you the time and assistance necessary to help you find the right home

- Proven experts in foreclosure and short sale properties (50% to 70% of the market in some areas)

Once again, do your research with co-workers, friends, family and business associates. You should even ask the lenders you are considering for a recommendation, as they are great resources for who knows what and who is doing a great job.

Upon finding the right agent, the next step will most likely not be yours; it will be the agent's. If the agent does not ask whether you are pre-approved during the first few minutes of getting to know you and your needs, get out of that office or car... fast! Know whether you have the wrong agent and need to move on.

If you take anything away from reading this book, understand that professional Realtors, in this day and age, will not put a buyer in their car, take time to review homes or spend any amount of time without:

- Having a letter or verbal confirmation from a loan officer *who they trust*

- Seeing that an application for a pre-approval has been submitted

- Confirming that you are qualified and ready to purchase

CHAPTER 11

Making the Offer

If this is your first time as a buyer, there is much to learn. If you are a return buyer, there are still things to bone up on, especially in light of the new types of sales such as "REOs," or "Real Estate Owned" (a fancy acronym for bank foreclosures) and "short sales."

Know the property you are buying

The first issue is to be sure you have done your homework. Before making the offer (and with the availability of today's technology) you should have gone to the town or county clerk's office to identify the tax situation and value applied to the property.

- How much are the taxes on that property?

- Is the property homesteaded? (Meaning a discount has been applied to the seller's tax bill, but will not be applied to yours until you meet the specific requirements of the state)

- Are there any liens on the property?

- (Most importantly) what is the estimated tax value— NOT market value, but tax value

Know the property's history

If you're online, you can drill down to see a property's past sales history. Questions to ask include:

- What do the current owners owe on the home?
- Are they maxed out at the asking price?
- Is there wiggle room?
- Are they underwater? (They owe more than the home is worth.)
- What did they purchase the property for and how long ago?

Next, ask your Realtor to show you comps (comparables) of similar homes in the area and start to form an idea around what your offer should be based on your research.

In today's environment and in many parts of the country, this is where the buying process becomes tricky. If you are in an area with many foreclosures, you will see that home prices are being hurt by empty homes, condos and short sales. Understand the market you are in and make offers accordingly.

NOTE: At the time of this writing, both the inventory of foreclosures and short sales have been declining at a rapid pace due to the many loan modification and refinancing options being offered to underwater homeowners.

Lastly, always beware of the seller looking to stick an unknowing buyer with their headache for a price well above market standards. This is a recipe for disaster, as today's appraisers do not mess around when it comes to being accurate. They also have a target on their backs and are not willing to risk their livelihood for one appraisal, simply to keep a Realtor or lender happy.

Realtors must deal with many sellers who are reluctant to accept that the value of their home has significantly decreased due to the meltdown, and that any increase in value will take a long time to recover. Many sellers will attempt to take advantage of inexperienced buyers—or those unaware of the market place—only to see the harsh reality of their dreams for selling high succumb to very conservative appraisals.

Understand seller-to-buyer sales

If you are buying a non-REO or short sale, you must do your homework and make a reasonable offer. Rely on the comps your Realtor has provided, and consider whether you want closing costs paid by the sellers. If you do, you can expect they will increase the sale price of the home—so hope the appraisal comes in satisfactorily. If it does, everyone is happy; if not, you'll have to consider renegotiation.

Seller-paid closing costs

Just a quick note on seller-paid closing costs. (Your Realtor will know about this, and if not, will refer you to a loan officer who certainly does.) There are two types of loans, *per se*, in the industry: Government loans and Conventional loans. Each has its own guidelines for seller-paid closing costs.

- Government loans are insured by the government and consist of loan programs such as FHA, VA and USDA.

- Conventional loans are typically referred to as those that Fannie Mae and Freddie Mac purchase from lenders.

Knowing which type of loan you are applying for is critical when making your offer, as the type of loan will indicate how much in seller-paid closing costs can be contributed: If an FHA loan, the contribution (as of this writing) is 6%; if you apply for a Conventional loan, the seller may pay up to 3%.

You must review the offer and the accepted contract

You cannot rely solely on the Realtor for this. You need as many sets of eyes on the offer and the final contract as possible. The most crucial step will be to identify the dates the parties have agreed to. You must be careful with three dates:

1. The commitment date, which is the date your loan must be approved

2. The application date, which typically requires the buyer to have submitted a loan application within five days

3. The closing date, which can cause unnecessary stress and anxiety when inserting an unrealistic (too short) date. Today's "normal" is 30 to 45 days, except with renovation loans such as the FHA 203K or Fannie Mae's renovation loan.

The other critical issue is the penalty clause. How many dollars per day will you pay for missing the closing date? Some buyers plan to miss it and have figured it in as part of the deal. Some of these penalties range from $50 to $100 per day.

Buyers must watch the commitment dates carefully, and recognize that lenders no longer provide actual commitment letters. Instead, they issue what are known as Conditional Commitments. These commitment letters do not provide a *full* approval, but rather an approval, which is subject to a number of items. These items could include borrower items, title items or others. What's important to understand is that the buyer must respond immediately with any information identified as "borrower items." Once the conditions are received, then accepted, the underwriter clears the file for closing.

Making the Offer—Review

1. You find a property you believe fits your needs.

2. With the Realtor's help, you research the home, its value, sales and mortgage history and tax status.

3. You create and review an offer, and attach a deposit check.

4. Upon acceptance, you review one last time (especially any changes to key dates).

5. If you have not submitted all supporting docs to your lender, it's imperative to do so now.

6. Prepare for the home inspection, obtain a survey and pest report (if applicable) and stay on top of your loan process. A good loan officer will do this for you.

NOTE: When the lender asks for something, do not attempt to debate the request—he or she is merely adhering to required guidelines. Simply get the information to your lender as fast as humanly possible. It's not <u>whether</u> you need to get the information: it's <u>how fast</u> you get the information to the lender and want to close the loan. There is no compromise in the mortgage arena today.

While certain requests will not make sense to you, getting your loan approval should. Lenders will ask for items that some borrowers seem to want to debate. This does no one any good and just prolongs the process. Loan officers and processors are there to do one thing, and that is to get loans closed.

CHAPTER 12

Components of the Mortgage Process

The process is not as difficult as it seems—*if* you know what to do! The steps involved—from getting a mortgage to closing on a property—are as follows:

Application

Typically a borrower has applied online or in person as a potential buyer through a pre-approval from the lender. In order to apply, you must have the following information:

- Full names and addresses of all buyers
- Photo IDs
- Social security numbers and dates of birth (DOBs) of all buyers
- Phone numbers and addresses for all properties owned
- Annual taxes and insurance figures for all properties owned

- Account numbers and amounts of all assets
  - Checking and savings
  - 401Ks
  - IRAs
  - All other statements

- A complete work history for the past 24 months, including part-time
  - Phone numbers
  - Addresses
  - Start dates and termination dates
  - Gross monthly income
  - W-2s and pay-stubs

- Current mortgage balances and values, if you own other properties

- Rental income, if any

- Two years of tax returns (all schedules)

Submission to Processing

This happens only when your loan officer has received all documentation. A good loan officer will review your loan application and supporting documentation, then submit the loan to the processor when satisfied he or she has all the information needed to create an approvable loan. (See Mortgage Checklist, at the end of this chapter.) The processor will review the file again to be certain the loan officer did not miss any details or documents. Loan applications submitted without all correct documentation only result in more requests and pestering. As a borrower, you must respond immediately to any of these requests if you want your loan to continue through the system.

Submission to Underwriting

When the processor believes all the missing items (if any) have been received, the loan is submitted to the underwriter. The underwriter will also review the file but this time, with an eye to the guidelines. The underwriter applies all new guidelines and checks the processor's and loan officer's work. If anything is deemed missing, you will be asked to respond—in fact if you wish to meet your contract dates you *must* respond. Do not wait until the next day or two days, as this will easily cost you a week! Treat every request as urgent.

Submission to Closing

Once the underwriter provides a commitment, be advised this will include several conditions for final approval *besides* what the underwriter is required to submit. Conditions for final approval may include title issues, homeowner's insurance or contract issues. As noted earlier, lenders no longer issue actual final approvals but rather Conditional Commitments specifying conditions that must be met before a "clear to close" may be issued. (See Chapter 13, Section 6 for more about Conditional Commitments.)

The reason lenders no longer issue final approval letters is due to the many moving parts of the deal—at any given time, something could cause it to fall apart. It may have nothing to do with you, the borrower, but rather there might be a title problem, or the inability to secure insurance. There are many variables, and issuing a final approval without covering all the bases does no one any good. Final approval in today's environment is when the paper work is signed, the checks are exchanged and the buyers have the new keys in their hands.

Regulators have created new rules that can stop a closing dead in its tracks. These rules have had a significant impact on the decision to issue a true approval letter, as they have instilled fear in personnel for possibly approving a loan that could somehow be singled out as a repurchase. In some cases, this is something that can collapse a small lender.

Closing

Once your file has been cleared, it moves to the closing department. A number of people will now be involved in preparing for the closing: the closing attorney or title company, the home insurer and the lender. All parties will work diligently to complete the final numbers, which will be inserted into what's known as a "HUD-1 Settlement Statement." This form identifies all credits from the sellers and costs to the buyers. It is the final document that identifies the final dollar amount you will need to bring to closing. The HUD statement is similar to your original Good Faith Estimate, which outlined an estimate of closing costs at the time you applied for your mortgage. New laws state that these two forms must match at closing—and if they do not match, there will be penalties.

NOTE: Buyers may no longer pay closing costs with a check; all funds must be wired. The closing agency will provide you with all information long before closing.

This is the final step in the process and results in the buyers and sellers leaving with nothing more than the opportunity to begin their new lives.

However, for the lenders, the process is far from over. One of the final tasks they must perform is a last review of all signed documents. This review, as well as any subsequent examinations, is explained in one of the forms you will sign at closing. If the lenders determine that any information is missing from your documentation, you will be required to respond in order to finalize the deal.

If any corrections are required after the closing, you as the borrower will be responsible for complying with any and all requests to correct inaccuracies or errors by the lender. The simplest error, such as a missing signature, requires the borrower's full cooperation.

Mortgage Checklist

Review the following checklist carefully.

All items may not apply to your situation.

❏ INCOME: Two years of W-2s for all borrowers (if salaried)

INCOME: Last two years of tax returns signed with **all pages.**

INCOME: 30 days of **consistent** paystubs for all borrowers. Include a year-to-date paystub showing name of employer and borrower's name and Social Security number.

Or if you receive Social Security payments or income from investments or Trust, include documentation to show the income. For Social Security income, use your annual award letter. For pensions that pay on a continual basis, use your most recent statement **or** tax returns for the past two years showing the income.

Or if you receive income from an annuity, you need to show that this income stream will last for a minimum of three years. To achieve this, send a statement and a letter from your financial planner or manager of the account. You will also need to provide two years of tax returns showing the monies received during each year.

❏ ASSETS: The asset requirement is to identify the source of funds for your down payment and closing costs. Include two months of every asset statement: checking, savings, 401k, pension, etc. **Include all pages of every statement (including blank pages).**

❏ LARGE DEPOSITS: An explanation of any deposits other than normal that show up on your bank statements. Go through your statement before you send. If there are larger than normal or random deposits, identify what they are for; where or who they came from; and any documentation to support the deposit. Upon review, you may need to provide additional documentation showing the source of deposits.

❏ IDENTITY: Copies of two forms of identity. A Social Security card is required for FHA loans. A driver's license or passport is required for all loans. **Please enlarge and lighten copies so that they are legible.**

❏ MULTIPLE PROPERTIES OR RENTALS: If you own other properties, provide a current mortgage statement, tax bill, and insurance bill showing annual costs for each.

❏ INQUIRIES ON YOUR CREDIT REPORT: You will be asked to sign a form explaining any recent inquiries on your credit report. Your loan officer will provide this form to you. You must explain what the inquiry was for; whether any new accounts were opened; and/or whether any new debt has been incurred due to new inquiries. If new debt has been incurred, you must explain the new terms and conditions of the debt such as payments, limits, and interest rates.

❏ INSURANCE INFO: Name and contact information of person responsible for securing homeowner's insurance on the new home. **(You may provide later if this is a new purchase.)** Upon choosing an insurer, contact your loan officer or processor with the name and contact information of your insurance agent. If a refinance, you must forward your declaration page showing the annual premium.

❏ CONTACT INFO: Name and contact information of the title company or attorney's office responsible for closing the loan; and all contact information for all Realtors involved. **(Your Realtor will provide this information.)**

❏ CONTRACT DEPOSIT: Copy of your deposit check. You will need to update this with a bank verification showing that the check cleared your account. **(Your Realtor can usually provide a copy of the deposit check.)**

❏ SURVEY: All states have their own rules for surveys. In some states, a waiver is allowed while others, such as Florida, require a survey (with the exception of condos). Submit the survey to the title company, attorney's office, or closing company.

❏ APPRAISAL: To cover appraisal costs, a credit card number is required on file for all purchases and refinances.

CHAPTER 13

Walking Through a Loan Application

Now we'll review the eight steps in the life of processing your loan.

1. The Offer

First, you negotiated a contract offer on a home you believe fits your requirements; you've researched the neighborhood, the schools, travel time for work and the functionality of the home. Your next decision is what to offer. This is a critical step, as you must consider that other offers may be coming in, especially if the property is a foreclosure or short sale.

To put forth the correct offer, you will need to consider a few options:

    1. Do you need the seller to pay closing costs?

    2. Do you know the home values in the neighborhood?

    3. Has your Realtor searched out other comparable properties that have recently sold in that neighborhood?

Once you have answered these questions, you and your agent can make an informed decision.

2. The Deposit

Along with your offer, you will provide the Realtor with a deposit on the home. The Realtor will forward the deposit check to the closing agency (title company or attorney, depending on which state you are in).

3. The Complete Loan Application

The contract will dictate that you have a certain number of days to apply for your mortgage. Since you have already been pre-approved, you need only update the loan officer with the property's address and complete the loan (if not yet completed).

There is, however, more to this step than meets the eye.

A *complete* loan application is the foundation for approval. During the pre-approval stage you will have provided the basic information necessary to receive the pre-approval letter. Now that you have a contract on a home, you will need to complete all the small details on the loan application (known as the "1003"). The loan officer will now need to include personal facts, such as the number of years you attended school (grade 1 through college) and whether you have children (including their ages). All work details (start dates, end dates and monthly gross earnings) and copies of tax bills, insurance bills and mortgage statements for every property you own must also be included. (See Mortgage Loan Application at the end of this chapter.)

All of these little details must be included on the application prior to your signing, for one important reason: *The loan application is a legal document.* Everything you include must be the truth to the best of your knowledge—and you will be legally responsible for the veracity of all information when you sign your name to that document.

Upon receipt of all information, the loan officer will provide you with multiple documents for your signature. These must be signed quickly and returned, along with any outstanding documentation that the loan officer identifies. This may include most recent W-2s, pay stubs, bank statements, tax returns, letters of explanation or any other requests that the loan officer deems pertinent to getting approval for your loan.

Once you have returned all documents, the loan officer will review it for missing information. If nothing is missing, the loan will be submitted to processing, where the loan processor will again review. If nothing is missing, the loan will be submitted to underwriting.

NOTE: Very rarely does a loan survive a loan officer and processor's review without some documentation or supporting information identified as missing by the underwriter. As a borrower, there is no need to be alarmed as there are so many circumstances related to each file that it's nearly impossible to escape the need for more information. Respond quickly, and the process will work.

4. Submission to Processor

Once the file is submitted to the processor, two things happen:

1. The appraisal will be ordered
   (which you will be required to pay for with a credit card).

2. The title will be ordered.

NOTE: The processor is your best friend. A good processor may appear to be overbearing, or ask for information that may not make sense. I strongly recommend that you do not fight the processor's requests! Embrace his or her attention to detail, as he or she knows better than anyone else on the planet what it takes to get your loan approved with as little inconvenience to you, the borrower, as humanly possible.

5. Borrower's Responsibilities

At the same time the file is submitted for loan processing, a borrower should be focused on the inspection of the home, if necessary. Home inspections identify potential problems and expose issues or concerns you may not have seen while walking through the home. Typical costs for home inspections are $350 to $500, depending on the area in which you live. The Realtor generally assists and can even recommend a reputable inspector. If any pest inspections are required, those are performed in conjunction with the home inspection.

The borrower's next action is to schedule a survey for the home (depending on lender requirements, as every state is different). If your lender requires a survey, check with your Realtor for a qualified professional. The costs again depend on the area in which you live, and can range between $350 and $500.

Lastly, this is also the time to begin shopping for a homeowner's policy, which must be paid-in-full for the first year prior to closing.

6. Submission to Underwriter

After the processor receives the appraisal, reviews the documents for accuracy and verifies the property value, the file will be sent to the underwriter, who again reviews the entire loan file and applies specific guidelines for the selected loan. The underwriter will then issue a Conditional Commitment. This is a list of what the underwriter believes is necessary to complete the loan approval. In some cases, this list has only to do with title issues, while in other cases it could require further information from you, the borrower.

Remember our earlier discussion about how employees in the lending industry all have targets on their backs, from both the regulators and the big lenders like Fannie Mae and the Big Four banks? For this reason, your file will be reviewed with a fine-tooth comb to ensure that it meets the requirements implemented by these institutions. Failure to produce a quality file will result in a repurchase of the loan by the lender.

This repurchase demand will only allow a lender to correct any errors within 30 days or the loan must be repurchased with *cash*. This is serious business when one considers that Fannie, Freddie and the big banks are putting thousands of demands on lenders. As a borrower, it is critical to understand why you are being asked certain questions, which may appear to be unusual. It's not because your lender does not want to make the loan (as the media would have you believe); it's because the big guys are out to recoup losses (Fannie and Freddie) and to also insure themselves against new borrower defaults.

NOTE: A huge rise in new FHA loan defaults in just the past three years suggests that guidelines, such as for minimum down payments, need tightening.

7. Final Approval

Once you receive final approval, the underwriter refers the loan to the closing department. The closers then coordinate with the closing company, which will be either a title company or a local attorney who will verify all figures for closing. They will also be sure that the documentation necessary for signing by both sellers and buyers complies with the laws of lending. Upon agreement by all parties, everyone involved will be notified of the date for closing.

The borrower will then receive a final document called the HUD-1 Settlement Statement. This is the document that ties all the costs of the home purchase together. (See HUD-1 Settlement Statement at the end of this chapter.) The form identifies the purchase price of the home, minus the loan amount approved by the lender, minus any seller-paid closing costs, minus any borrower deposits, plus any taxes due by buyer and/or other fees. The bottom line reflects the amount of cash necessary for the closing to take place and for the keys to be handed over.

8. Closing Day!

Finally, your day has arrived. Prior to this day you will have been advised to wire transfer the funds to the closing firm in order to cover the closing costs. At the closing table, the closing agent will put before you one more stack of papers, and begin going through them one at a time with an explanation of each form's purpose. The HUD-1 Settlement Statement is typically the first form you will see in order to verify that the figures you expected at closing were correct.

Uniform Residential Loan Application

This application is designed to be completed by the applicant(s) with the Lender's assistance. Applicants should complete this form as "Borrower" or "Co-Borrower," as applicable. Co-Borrower information must also be provided (and the appropriate box checked) when ☐ the income or assets of a person other than the Borrower (including the Borrower's spouse) will be used as a basis for loan qualification or ☐ the income or assets of the Borrower's spouse or other person who has community property rights pursuant to state law will not be used as a basis for loan qualification, but his or her liabilities must be considered because the spouse or other person has community property rights pursuant to applicable law and Borrower resides in a community property state, the security property is located in a community property state, or the Borrower is relying on other property located in a community property state as a basis for repayment of the loan.

If this is an application for joint credit, Borrower and Co-Borrower each agree that we intend to apply for joint credit (sign below):

Borrower _____

Co-Borrower _____

I. TYPE OF MORTGAGE AND TERMS OF LOAN

Mortgage Applied for:	☐ VA ☐ Conventional ☐ Other (explain): ☐ FHA ☐ USDA/Rural Housing Service		Agency Case Number	Lender Case Number
Amount $	Interest Rate %	No. of Months	Amortization Type: ☐ Fixed Rate ☐ Other (explain): ☐ GPM ☐ ARM (type):	

II. PROPERTY INFORMATION AND PURPOSE OF LOAN

Subject Property Address (street, city, state & ZIP) — No. of Units

Legal Description of Subject Property (attach description if necessary) — Year Built

Purpose of Loan	☐ Purchase ☐ Construction ☐ Other (explain): ☐ Refinance ☐ Construction-Permanent	Property will be: ☐ Primary Residence ☐ Secondary Residence ☐ Investment

Complete this line if construction or construction-permanent loan.

Year Lot Acquired	Original Cost $	Amount Existing Liens $	(a) Present Value of Lot $	(b) Cost of Improvements	Total (a + b) $

Complete this line if this is a refinance loan.

Year Acquired	Original Cost $	Amount Existing Liens $	Purpose of Refinance	Describe Improvements ☐ made ☐ to be made	
				Cost: $	

Title will be held in what Name(s) — Manner in which Title will be held — Estate will be held in: ☐ Fee Simple ☐ Leasehold (show expiration date)

Source of Down Payment, Settlement Charges, and/or Subordinate Financing (explain)

III. BORROWER INFORMATION

	Borrower	Co-Borrower
Borrower's Name (include Jr. or Sr. if applicable)		Co-Borrower's Name (include Jr. or Sr. if applicable)

Social Security Number	Home Phone (incl. area code)	DOB (mm/dd/yyyy)	Yrs. School	Social Security Number	Home Phone (incl. area code)	DOB (mm/dd/yyyy)	Yrs. School

☐ Married ☐ Unmarried (include single, divorced, widowed) ☐ Separated	Dependents (not listed by Co-Borrower) no. ages	☐ Married ☐ Unmarried (include single, divorced, widowed) ☐ Separated	Dependents (not listed by Borrower) no. ages

Present Address (street, city, state, ZIP) ☐ Own ☐ Rent ___ No. Yrs. | Present Address (street, city, state, ZIP) ☐ Own ☐ Rent ___ No. Yrs.

Mailing Address, if different from Present Address | Mailing Address, if different from Present Address

If residing at present address for less than two years, complete the following:

Former Address (street, city, state, ZIP) ☐ Own ☐ Rent ___ No. Yrs. | Former Address (street, city, state, ZIP) ☐ Own ☐ Rent ___ No. Yrs.

IV. EMPLOYMENT INFORMATION

	Borrower	Co-Borrower

Name & Address of Employer ☐ Self Employed	Yrs. on this job	Name & Address of Employer ☐ Self Employed	Yrs. on this job
	Yrs. employed in this line of work/profession		Yrs. employed in this line of work/profession
Position/Title/Type of Business	Business Phone (incl. area code)	Position/Title/Type of Business	Business Phone (incl. area code)

If employed in current position for less than two years or if currently employed in more than one position, complete the following:

Name & Address of Employer ☐ Self Employed	Dates (from - to)	Name & Address of Employer ☐ Self Employed	Dates (from - to)
	Monthly Income $		Monthly Income $
Position/Title/Type of Business	Business Phone (incl. area code)	Position/Title/Type of Business	Business Phone (incl. area code)
Name & Address of Employer ☐ Self Employed	Dates (from - to)	Name & Address of Employer ☐ Self Employed	Dates (from - to)
	Monthly Income $		Monthly Income $
Position/Title/Type of Business	Business Phone (incl. area code)	Position/Title/Type of Business	Business Phone (incl. area code)

Freddie Mac Form 65 7/05
Fannie Mae Form 1003 7/05
VMP-21N (0507) NMFL #1003N (APR1-APR2) Rev. 11/14/2005

V. MONTHLY INCOME AND COMBINED HOUSING EXPENSE INFORMATION

Gross Monthly Income	Borrower	Co-Borrower	Total	Combined Monthly Housing Expense	Present	Proposed
Base Empl. Income*	$	$	$	Rent	$	
Overtime				First Mortgage (P&I)		$
Bonuses				Other Financing (P&I)		
Commissions				Hazard Insurance		
Dividends/Interest				Real Estate Taxes		
Net Rental Income				Mortgage Insurance		
Other (before completing, see the notice in "describe other income," below)				Homeowner Assn. Dues		
				Other:		
Total	$	$	$	Total	$	$

* Self Employed Borrower(s) may be required to provide additional documentation such as tax returns and financial statements.

Describe Other Income   Notice: Alimony, child support, or separate maintenance income need not be revealed if the Borrower (B) or Co-Borrower (C) does not choose to have it considered for repaying this loan.

B/C		Monthly Amount
		$

VI. ASSETS AND LIABILITIES

This Statement and any applicable supporting schedules may be completed jointly by both married and unmarried Co-Borrowers if their assets and liabilities are sufficiently joined so that the Statement can be meaningfully and fairly presented on a combined basis; otherwise, separate Statements and Schedules are required. If the Co-Borrower section was completed about a non-applicant spouse or other person, this statement and supporting schedules must be completed about that spouse or other person also.

Completed ☐ Jointly ☐ Not Jointly

SAMPLE

ASSETS Description	Cash or Market Value	LIABILITIES	Monthly Payment & Months Left to Pay	Unpaid Balance
Cash deposit toward purchase held by:	$	Liabilities and Pledged Assets. List the creditor's name, address, and account number for all outstanding debts, including automobile loans, revolving charge accounts, real estate loans, alimony, child support, stock pledges, etc. Use continuation sheet, if necessary. Indicate by (*) those liabilities, which will be satisfied upon sale of real estate owned or upon refinancing of the subject property.		
List checking and savings accounts below		Name and address of Company	$ Payment/Months	$
Name and address of Bank, S&L, or Credit Union				
		Acct. no.		
Acct. no.	$	Name and address of Company	$ Payment/Months	$
Name and address of Bank, S&L, or Credit Union				
		Acct. no.		
Acct. no.	$	Name and address of Company	$ Payment/Months	$
Name and address of Bank, S&L, or Credit Union				
		Acct. no.		
Acct. no.	$	Name and address of Company	$ Payment/Months	$
Name and address of Bank, S&L, or Credit Union				
		Acct. no.		
Acct. no.	$	Name and address of Company	$ Payment/Months	$
Stocks & Bonds (Company name/number & description)	$			
		Acct. no.		
		Name and address of Company	$ Payment/Months	$
Life insurance net cash value	$			
Face amount: $				
Subtotal Liquid Assets	$			
Real estate owned (enter market value from schedule of real estate owned)	$	Acct. no.		
Vested interest in retirement fund	$	Name and address of Company	$ Payment/Months	$
Net worth of business(es) owned (attach financial statement)	$			
Automobiles owned (make and year)	$			
		Acct. no.		
		Alimony/Child Support/Separate Maintenance Payments Owed to:	$	
Other Assets (itemize)	$	Job-Related Expense (child care, union dues, etc.)	$	
		Total Monthly Payments	$	
Total Assets a.	$	Net Worth ▶ (a minus b) $	Total Liabilities b.	$

VI. ASSETS AND LIABILITIES (cont'd)

Schedule of Real Estate Owned (If additional properties are owned, use continuation sheet.)

Property Address (enter S if sold, PS if pending sale or R if rental being held for income) ▼	Type of Property	Present Market Value	Amount of Mortgages & Liens	Gross Rental Income	Mortgage Payments	Insurance, Maintenance, Taxes & Misc.	Net Rental Income
		$	$	$	$	$	$
Totals		$	$	$	$	$	$

List any additional names under which credit has previously been received and indicate appropriate creditor name(s) and account number(s):

Alternate Name	Creditor Name	Account Number

VII. DETAILS OF TRANSACTION

a. Purchase price	$
b. Alterations, improvements, repairs	
c. Land (if acquired separately)	
d. Refinance (incl. debts to be paid off)	
e. Estimated prepaid items	
f. Estimated closing costs	
g. PMI, MIP, Funding Fee	
h. Discount (if Borrower will pay)	
i. Total costs (add items a through h)	
j. Subordinate financing	
k. Borrower's closing costs paid by Seller	
l. Other Credits (explain)	
m. Loan amount (exclude PMI, MIP, Funding Fee financed)	
n. PMI, MIP, Funding Fee financed	
o. Loan amount (add m & n)	
p. Cash from/to Borrower (subtract j, k, l & o from i)	

VIII. DECLARATIONS

If you answer "Yes" to any questions a through i, please use continuation sheet for explanation.

	Borrower		Co-Borrower	
	Yes	No	Yes	No
a. Are there any outstanding judgments against you?	☐	☐	☐	☐
b. Have you been declared bankrupt within the past 7 years?	☐	☐	☐	☐
c. Have you had property foreclosed upon or given title or deed in lieu thereof in the last 7 years?	☐	☐	☐	☐
d. Are you a party to a lawsuit?	☐	☐	☐	☐
e. Have you directly or indirectly been obligated on any loan which resulted in foreclosure, transfer of title in lieu of foreclosure, or judgment? (This would include such loans as home mortgage loans, SBA loans, home improvement loans, educational loans, manufactured (mobile) home loans, any mortgage, financial obligation, bond, or loan guarantee. If "Yes," provide details, including date, name, and address of Lender, FHA or VA case number, if any, and reasons for the action.)	☐	☐	☐	☐
f. Are you presently delinquent or in default on any Federal debt or any other loan, mortgage, financial obligation, bond, or loan guarantee? If "Yes," give details as described in the preceding question.	☐	☐	☐	☐
g. Are you obligated to pay alimony, child support, or separate maintenance?	☐	☐	☐	☐
h. Is any part of the down payment borrowed?	☐	☐	☐	☐
i. Are you a co-maker or endorser on a note?	☐	☐	☐	☐
j. Are you a U.S. citizen?	☐	☐	☐	☐
k. Are you a permanent resident alien?	☐	☐	☐	☐
l. Do you intend to occupy the property as your primary residence? If "Yes," complete question m below.	☐	☐	☐	☐
m. Have you had an ownership interest in a property in the last three years?	☐	☐	☐	☐
(1) What type of property did you own - - principal residence (PR), second home (SH), or investment property (IP)?				
(2) How did you hold title to the home - - solely by yourself (S), jointly with your spouse (SP), or jointly with another person (O)?				

IX. ACKNOWLEDGEMENT AND AGREEMENT

Each of the undersigned specifically represents to Lender and to Lender's actual or potential agents, brokers, processors, attorneys, insurers, servicers, successors and assigns and agrees and acknowledges that: (1) the information provided in this application is true and correct as of the date set forth opposite my signature and that any intentional or negligent misrepresentation of this information contained in this application may result in civil liability, including monetary damages, to any person who may suffer any loss due to reliance upon any misrepresentation that I have made on this application, and/or in criminal penalties including, but not limited to, fine or imprisonment or both under the provisions of Title 18, United States Code, Sec. 1001, et seq.; (2) the loan requested pursuant to this application (the "Loan") will be secured by a mortgage or deed of trust on the property described in this application; (3) the property will not be used for any illegal or prohibited purpose or use; (4) all statements made in this application are made for the purpose of obtaining a residential mortgage loan; (5) the property will be occupied as indicated in this application; (6) the Lender, its servicers, successors or assigns may retain the original and/or an electronic record of this application, whether or not the Loan is approved; (7) the Lender and its agents, brokers, insurers, servicers, successors, and assigns may continuously rely on the information contained in the application, and I am obligated to amend and/or supplement the information provided in this application if any of the material facts that I have represented herein should change prior to closing of the Loan; (8) in the event that my payments on the Loan become delinquent, the Lender, its servicers, successors or assigns may, in addition to any other rights and remedies that it may have relating to such delinquency, report my name and account information to one or more consumer reporting agencies; (9) ownership of the Loan and/or administration of the Loan account may be transferred with such notice as may be required by law; (10) neither Lender nor its agents, brokers, insurers, servicers, successors or assigns has made any representation or warranty, express or implied, to me regarding the property or the condition or value of the property; and (11) my transmission of this application as an "electronic record" containing my "electronic signature," as those terms are defined in applicable federal and/or state laws (excluding audio and video recordings), or my facsimile transmission of this application containing a facsimile of my signature, shall be as effective, enforceable and valid as if a paper version of this application were delivered containing my original written signature.

Acknowledgement. Each of the undersigned hereby acknowledges that any owner of the Loan, its servicers, successors and assigns, may verify or reverify any information contained in this application or obtain any information or data relating to the Loan, for any legitimate business purpose through any source, including a source named in this application or a consumer reporting agency.

Borrower's Signature	Date	Co-Borrower's Signature	Date
X		X	

X. INFORMATION FOR GOVERNMENT MONITORING PURPOSES

The following information is requested by the Federal Government for certain types of loans related to a dwelling in order to monitor the lender's compliance with equal credit opportunity, fair housing and home mortgage disclosure laws. You are not required to furnish this information, but are encouraged to do so. The law provides that a lender may not discriminate either on the basis of this information, or on whether you choose to furnish it. If you furnish the information, please provide both ethnicity and race. For race, you may check more than one designation. If you do not furnish ethnicity, race, or sex, under Federal regulations, this lender is required to note the information on the basis of visual observation and surname if you have made this application in person. If you do not wish to furnish the information, please check the box below. (Lender must review the above material to assure that the disclosures satisfy all requirements to which the lender is subject under applicable state law for the particular type of loan applied for.)

BORROWER ☐ I do not wish to furnish this information.	CO-BORROWER ☐ I do not wish to furnish this information.
Ethnicity: ☐ Hispanic or Latino ☐ Not Hispanic or Latino	**Ethnicity:** ☐ Hispanic or Latino ☐ Not Hispanic or Latino
Race: ☐ American Indian or Alaska Native ☐ Asian ☐ Black or African American ☐ Native Hawaiian or Other Pacific Islander ☐ White	**Race:** ☐ American Indian or Alaska Native ☐ Asian ☐ Black or African American ☐ Native Hawaiian or Other Pacific Islander ☐ White
Sex: ☐ Female ☐ Male	**Sex:** ☐ Female ☐ Male

To be Completed by Interviewer This application was taken by:	Interviewer's Name (print or type)	Name and Address of Interviewer's Employer
☐ Face-to-face interview		
☐ Mail	Interviewer's Signature Date	
☐ Telephone		
☐ Internet	Interviewer's Phone Number (incl. area code)	

CONTINUATION SHEET/RESIDENTIAL LOAN APPLICATION		
Use this continuation sheet if you need more space to complete the Residential Loan Application. Mark B for Borrower or C for Co-Borrower.	Borrower:	Agency Case Number:
	Co-Borrower:	Lender Case Number:

SAMPLE

California applicants: Under California Civil Code 1812.30(j), credit applications for the obtainment of money, goods, labor, or services shall clearly specify that the applicant, if married, may apply for a separate account.

I/We fully understand that it is a Federal crime punishable by fine or imprisonment, or both, to knowingly make any false statements concerning any of the above facts as applicable under the provisions of Title 18, United States Code, Section 1001, et seq.

Borrower's Signature:	Date	Co-Borrower's Signature:	Date
X		X	

HUD-1

A. Settlement Statement (HUD-1)

OMB Approval No. 2502-0265

B. Type of Loan

○ 1. FHA	○ 2. RHS	● 3. Conv. Unins.	**6. File Number** File No 123	**7. Loan Number** 2222861 ID:	**8. Mortg. Ins. Case Num.**
○ 4. V.A.	○ 5. Conv. Ins.				

C. NOTE: This form is furnished to give you a statement of actual settlement costs. Amounts paid to and by the settlement agent are shown. Items marked "(p.o.c.)" were paid outside the closing; they are shown here for informational purposes and are not included in the totals.

D. NAME OF BORROWER:	John Smith Buyer and Sally Smith Buyer
Address of Borrower:	342 Glenwood Avenue, Sarasota, Florida 34232
E. NAME OF SELLER:	Martin Jones Seller and Betty Jones Seller
Address of Seller:	1528 Applegate, Bradenton, Florida 34205
F. NAME OF LENDER:	Academy Mortgage Corporation
Address of Lender:	1615 South Federal Highway, 100, Boca Raton, Florida 33432
G. PROPERTY LOCATION:	4455 Pineapple Drive, Sarasota, Florida 34241
H. SETTLEMENT AGENT:	Longboat Title Services, L.C.
Place of Settlement:	6350 Gulf of Mexico Drive, Suite 103, Longboat Key, Florida 34228 Phone: 941-387-8773
I. SETTLEMENT DATE:	8/20/12 ISBU OF MEN DATE 3/20/12

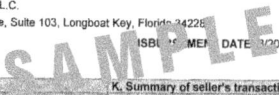

J. Summary of borrower's transaction		K. Summary of seller's transaction	
100. Gross amount due from borrower:		**400. Gross amount due to seller:**	
101. Contract sales price	150,000.00	401. Contract sales price	150,000.00
102. Personal property		402. Personal property	
103. Settlement charges to borrower (Line 1400)	7,525.66	403.	
104.		404.	
105.		405.	
Adjustments for items paid by seller in advance:		**Adjustments for items paid by seller in advance:**	
106. City/town taxes		406. City/town taxes	
107. County taxes		407. County taxes	
108. HOA Maint Dues from 07/01/12 to 12/31/12	250.00	408. HOA Maint Dues from 07/01/12 to 12/31/12	250.00
109.		409.	
110.		410.	
111.		411.	
112.		412.	
120. Gross amount due from borrower:	157,775.66	**420. Gross amount due to seller:**	150,250.00
200. Amounts paid or in behalf of borrower:		**500. Reductions in amount due to seller:**	
201. Deposit or earnest money	5,000.00	501. Excess deposit (see instructions)	
202. Principal amount of new loan(s)	120,000.00	502. Settlement charges to seller (line 1400)	9,000.00
203. Existing loan(s) taken subject to		503. Existing loan(s) taken subject to	
204. Principal amount of second mortgage		504. Payoff of first mortgage loan	
205.		505. Payoff of second mortgage loan	
206.		506.	
207.		507. Deposit is being disbursed as proceeds	
208. Principal amt of mortgage held by seller		508. Principal amt of mortgage held by seller	
209.		509.	
209a.		509a.	
Adjustments for items unpaid by seller:		**Adjustments for items unpaid by seller:**	
210. City/town taxes		510. City/town taxes	
211. 2012 County taxes from 01/01/12 to 08/20/12	1,521.32	511. 2012 County taxes from 01/01/12 to 08/20/12	1,521.32
212. Assessments		512. Assessments	
213.		513.	
214.		514.	
215.		515.	
216.		516.	
217.		517.	
218.		518.	
219.		519.	
220. Total paid by/for borrower:	126,521.32	**520. Total reductions in amount due seller:**	10,521.32
300. Cash at settlement from/to borrower:		**600. Cash at settlement to/from seller:**	
301. Gross amount due from borrower (line 120)	157,775.66	601. Gross amount due to seller (line 420)	150,250.00
302. Less amount paid by/for the borrower (line 220)	(126,521.32)	602. Less total reductions in amount due seller (line 520)	(10,521.32)
303. Cash (✓ From ☐ To) Borrower:	31,254.34	603. Cash (✓ To ☐ From) Seller:	139,728.68

Borrower's Initial(s):

Seller's Initial(s):

DoubleTime®

HUD-1   U.S. Department of Housing and Urban Development   Page 2

L. Settlement charges			Paid from Borrower's Funds at Settlement	Paid from Seller's Funds at Settlement
700. Total Real Estate Broker Fees **$9,000.00**				
Division of commission (line 700) as follows:				
701. $ 4,500.00	to	Real Estate Company		
702. $ 4,500.00	to	Realty, Inc		
703. Commission paid at settlement				9,000.00
704.				
705.	to			
800. Items Payable in Connection with Loan				
801. Our origination charge		$1,090.00 (from GFE #1)		
802. Your credit or charge (points) for the specific interest rate chosen		(from GFE #2)		
803. Your adjusted origination charges	to Academy Mortgage Corporation	(from GFE A)	1,090.00	
804. Appraisal fee	to Appraisal Group	(from GFE #3)	375.00	
805. Credit report	to Equifax	(from GFE #3)	20.00	
806. Tax service	to	(from GFE #3)		
807. Flood certification	to	(from GFE #3)		
808.	to			
809.	to			
810.	to			
811.	to			
812.	to			
813.	to			
900. Items Required by Lender to Be Paid in Advance				
901. Daily interest charges from 08/20/12 to 09. 2 @ 12.3300 /day (from GFE #10)			147.96	
902. Mortgage insurance premium for months to		(from GFE #3)		
903. Homeowner's insurance premium years to Florida Insurance Company		(from GFE #11)	1,200.96	
904. HO6 insurance premium for years to				
905.	years to			
1000. Reserves Deposited with Lender				
1001. Initial deposit for your escrow account		(from GFE #9)	700.24	
1002. Homeowner's insurance 3 months @ $100.08 per month $300.24				
1003. Mortgage insurance months @ per month				
1004. Property taxes 3 months @ $200.00 per month $600.00				
1005. Flood insurance months @ per month				
1006. HO6 Ins months @ per month				
1007. months @ per month				
1008. months @ per month				
1009. Aggregate accounting adjustment		($200.00)		
1100. Title Charges				
1101. Title services and lender's title insurance		(from GFE #4)	882.50	
1102. Settlement or closing fee	to Longboat Title Services, L.C. $400.00			
1103. Owner's title insurance	to Longboat Title Services, L.C.	(from GFE #5)	825.00	
OF6-825.00				
1104. Lender's title insurance	to Longboat Title Services, L.C.	$407.50		
MF6-250.00;5.1-25;8.1-25;F9-107.50				
1105. Lender's title policy limit $120,000.00				
1106. Owner's title policy limit $150,000.00				
1107. Agent's portion of the total title insurance premium $862.75	to Longboat Title Services, L.C.			
1108. Underwriter's portion of the total title insurance premium $369.75	to Longboat Title Services, L.C.			
1109. Abstract or title search	to Longboat Title Services, L.C. $75.00			
1110.	to			
1111.	to			
1112.	to			
1113.	to			
1200. Government Recording and Transfer Charges				
1201. Government recording charges		(from GFE #7)	224.00	
1202. Deed $18.50 Mortgage(s) $205.50 Releases $0.00		$224.00		
1203. Transfer taxes		(from GFE #8)	1,710.00	
1204. City/County tax/stamps Deed $0.00 Mortgage(s) $240.00				
1205. State tax/stamps Deed $1,050.00 Mortgage(s) $420.00				
1206.				
1207.				
1208.				
1300. Additional Settlement Charges				
1301. Required services that you can shop for		(from GFE #6)	350.00	
1302. Survey	to Residential Land Services $350.00			
1303.	to			
1304.	to			
1305.	to			
1306.	to			
1307.	to			
1308.	to			
1309.				
1400. Total Settlement Charges				
(Enter on lines 103, Section J and 502, Section K.)			7,525.66	9,000.00

* POC (B) = Paid outside of closing by borrower
* POC (S) = Paid outside of closing by seller

Borrower's Initial(s):   Seller's Initial(s):

DoubleTime®

D DOUBLETIME®

08/20/12 02:33 PM

Closing File Number: File No 123

801 Origination Statement

Loan Processing Fee $595.00
Underwriting Fee $495.00

Itemized Origination Fees and Charges Total: $1,090.00
(Line 801 amount)

SAMPLE

Borrower(s)

John Smith Buyer

By: _____ Date: _____

CHAPTER 14

Standard Requirements for Obtaining a Mortgage

In this section we will outline the general "minimum" requirements. Though these minimums can vary under certain circumstances— such as for a college student who is just entering the workplace, or a veteran returning from war—for the most part you can rest assured the minimums will not change.

Following are the minimums listed by category:

1. Employment – a consistent history of 24 months, or explanation for gaps

2. Income – 30 days of consistent pay stubs and W-2s for salaried workers, or:

   a. Self-Employed – two years of tax returns without losses

   b. Retirement Income – pension letters and Social Security income letters

3. Assets – consistent statements for the last 60 days. Statements must include all pages.

4. Ratios – cannot exceed the stipulated guides for the loan program (i.e., FHA loans 50%, Conventional loans 45%)

5. Credit scores – cannot be below 640
   NOTE: Some lenders state they will work with you if your credit score is lower, but the reality is that very few get approved. No investor wants to purchase such low-grade paper.

6. Previous bankruptcy, foreclosure, short sale, loan modification documentation. (See Bankruptcy/ Foreclosure/Short-Sale/Loan Modification Grid at the end of this chapter.)

These are general guidelines that any lender will require you meet in order to consider you for a mortgage. It is not to be considered the complete list, as lenders may have layered other guidelines on top for their own organizations. For instance, just because FHA states it will write a loan for a borrower with a credit score of 500, 99% of all lenders will not touch the loan due to risk and liability reasons.

One last point is that many borrowers save and save for their purchase without an estimate of how much it will cost to close. Read closely, as this is the one component that bites buyers in the butt in today's market. In addition to the down payment, every loan has certain closing cost fees that are paid to the state as taxes or state-imposed real estate fees. These closing fees can be as high as 4% to 5%, depending on your market. All loans generally include a processing and underwriting fee, appraisal and credit fee, closing fee, title insurance, state tax fees, survey fees and more.

Bottom line

Be prepared for more than a down payment. Always ask your loan officer for a quote on closing costs. (See Chapter 17 – Closing Costs.)

The Bankruptcy, Foreclosure, Short Sale, and Loan Modification Grid

Lenders review your past history as it relates to bankruptcy, foreclosure, deed-in-lieu (hand over the keys), loan modification, or short sale, based on either Conventional Loan Guidelines (Fannie Mae and Freddie Mac) or Government Loan Guidelines (FHA, VA, and USDA).

CONVENTIONAL LOAN GUIDELINES

Foreclosure – Pre-Foreclosure – Loan Modification – Short Sale:
7 years from the date foreclosure completed and transferred back to bank/lender.

For maximum financing allowed by the program:
- 4 years from the date foreclosure completed and transferred back to bank/lender with 10% down.
- 2 years from the date foreclosure completed and transferred back to bank/lender with 20% down.

Deed-in-Lieu of Foreclosure:
4 years from completion date for an owner-occupied purchase or limited cash out refinance. 7 years from completion date if transaction is a cash-out, second home, or investment property.

Loan Modifications:
Waiting period is from the modification completion date.

Bankruptcy Chapter 7:
4 years from date of discharge date or dismissal date.

Bankruptcy Chapter 13:
2 years from discharge date and 4 years from dismissal date.

Multiple Bankruptcy filings in 7 years:
5 years from latest discharge or dismissal date.

Consumer Credit Counseling:
Must be approved by the Fannie Mae or Freddie Mac automated systems.

GOVERNMENT LOAN GUIDELINES

FHA

Foreclosure - Deed-in-Lieu of Foreclosure:
3 years from the date foreclosure completed and transferred back to bank/lender,
Or Less than 3 years but not less than 12 months from the date foreclosure completed and transferred back to bank/lender may be acceptable if the result of extenuating circumstances.

Short Sale:
3 years from date sale closed and transferred to new owner.

Pre-Foreclosure:
Less than 3 years, but not less than 12 months when transferred back to bank/lender.

Loan Modification:
Waiting period is from the modification completion date.

Bankruptcy Chapter 7:
2 years from date of discharge with re-established credit paid as agreed or no new credit obligations incurred.

Bankruptcy Chapter 13:
1 year payout period under bankruptcy has elapsed and the borrower's payment performance has been satisfactory and all required payments made on time. Permission must be given by the courts to enter into a new mortgage obligation if currently under the payout period.

Consumer Credit Counseling:
1 year of the payout must have elapsed and payments must be made on time. Borrower must receive permission from the agency to enter into a mortgage.

VA Guidelines

Foreclosure - Deed-in-Lieu of Foreclosure:
2 years from date of foreclosure completed and transferred back to bank/lender.

Short-Sale:
2 years from date sale closed and transferred to new owner or completion date of modification.

Pre-Foreclosure:
Less than 3 years, but not less than 12 months when transferred back to bank/lender.

Loan Modification:
Waiting period is from the modification completion date.

Bankruptcy Chapter 7:
2 years from date of discharge or 12-23 months from date of discharge with re-established credit paid as agreed or no new credit obligations incurred

Bankruptcy Chapter 13:
1 year payout period under bankruptcy has elapsed and the borrower's payment performance has been satisfactory and all required payments made on time. Permission must be given by the courts to enter into a new mortgage obligation if currently under the payout period.

Consumer Credit Counseling:
1 year of the payout must have elapsed and payments must be made on time. Borrower must receive permission from the agency to enter into a mortgage

USDA Guidelines

Foreclosure - Deed-in-Lieu of Foreclosure:
3 years from date of foreclosure completed and transferred back to bank/lender.

Short Sale:
3 years from date sale closed and transferred to new owner or completion date of modification.

Pre-Foreclosure:
Less than 3 years, but not less than 12 months when transferred back to bank/lender.

Loan Modification:
Waiting period is from the modification completion date.

Bankruptcy Chapter 7:
3 years from date of discharge, 12-23 months from date of discharge with re-established credit paid as agreed or no new credit obligations incurred.

Bankruptcy Chapter 13:
1 year payout period under bankruptcy has elapsed and the borrower's payment performance has been satisfactory and all required payments made on time. Permission must be given by the courts to enter into a new mortgage obligation if currently under the payout period.

Consumer Credit Counseling:
1 year of the payout must have elapsed and payments must be made on time. Borrower must receive permission from the agency to enter into a mortgage.

CHAPTER 15

Understanding Mortgage Ratios

Mortgage ratios are used to identify a borrower's ability to repay the loan. Calculating ratios is a simple process, which I will show you later in this chapter. The calculation is nothing more than money you take in against money you pay out. If you receive $3,000 in gross monthly income and pay out $1,500 per month toward your mortgage, you are using a ratio of 50% of your income. Lenders have set benchmarks for borrowers to meet when it comes to how much they spend against their income.

There are two types of ratios lenders rely upon

Housing Ratio: This ratio consists of a new mortgage payment (principal and interest) along with other housing costs such as taxes, insurance or even flood insurance. If a condo or association, it may include a Home Owners Association Fee (HOA). Borrowers putting less than 20% down on a home will also need to add private mortgage insurance (PMI). Private mortgage insurance is paid monthly, and protects the lender in the event of a default.

These above fees are known as PITI: Principal, Interest, Taxes and Insurance. The housing ratio lenders typically look for is in the low to mid 30s. For example, Mr. Smith purchased a home for $150,000. His monthly PITI, plus association fee and private mortgage insurance is $1,100. He earns $3,500 per month. His housing ratio is calculated by dividing the PITI of $1,100 by his gross monthly income of $3,500 for a ratio of 31.42%.

Back Ratio: The second ratio is also referred to as "total debt." In this calculation, the borrower's total monthly payments for all revolving debt (credit cards), and installment loans (auto, student loans, other mortgages, etc.) are added to the new housing payment of PITI plus any other fees such as mortgage insurance or HOA. Once again, we use Mr. Smith as an example. We know he earns $3,500 gross monthly, and we know his new housing payment is $1,100. We now add $700 to his monthly housing payment for $1,800 in total monthly debt. Divide this figure ($1,800) by his gross income, and we have a total debt ratio of 51.14%.

Ratios differ among types of loans

While Mr. Smith may be over the typical ratio limit of 50%, qualifying for a loan will depend on the type of loan he is applying for. If an FHA loan, he may still qualify because he has strong credit and assets. If not, he will be declined. If the loan he applies for is a Conventional loan—meaning it must adhere to Fannie Mae and Freddie Mac guidelines—he is well over the ratio limit of 45%, but again this does not mean he won't qualify as he has strong compensating factors such as excellent credit and reserves. If he applies for a VA or USDA loan, he may again be declined as the ratios for those programs also differ.

For FHA, the ratios are flexible, although 50% of gross monthly income is standard. If you apply for a Conventional loan (Non-Government, not a Jumbo)—also known as a Fannie or Freddie loan—the guidelines state that you are allowed up to 45% of your gross monthly income to cover *all* monthly debt, including the new mortgage, taxes and insurance.

In another scenario, Mr. Jones is again buying a home for $150,000. He is using an FHA loan, which requires 3.5% down, and which will require private mortgage insurance due to the fact that he is putting less than 20% down. His payment on the new house will be roughly $1,100 and includes taxes, insurance, private mortgage insurance and an association fee. Mr. Jones earns $3,500 gross income on a monthly basis, and has monthly debt payments of $400 for credit card, auto and student loan payments.

To calculate his monthly housing ratio, we divide only the housing costs of $1,100 by his monthly gross income of $3,500. This gives us a ratio of 31%, which is well within the range of acceptability. The next calculation is the total debt-to-income. We add the monthly payments of $400 to the new loan payment of $1,100 and divide it again by his gross monthly income: $1100 + $400 = $1500/$3500 = 42%. Mr. Jones is well within the total allowable debt-to-income ratio of 50% for an FHA loan.

In our first scenario with Mr. Smith, where he was over the allowed rate of 50% of his gross monthly income and perhaps did not have ideal credit and assets, we would immediately begin reviewing his monthly debts to see what has been causing the failure. There are ways to improve his situation—for example, if he has less than 10 months to go on his car payment, we can eliminate this for consideration. Let's assume this is the case and that he pays $250 per month for the car. This drops his total monthly debt to $1,550, allowing him to pass the total debt-to-income requirement: $1550/$3500 = 44%.

Ratios sound complex, but they're not! Simply calculate your gross monthly income and divide your monthly debts by that amount. It's not rocket science, and it can help you identify where you stand before you call a lender or Realtor.

More important for the reader to grasp is this: There are so many different programs with varying ratios and guidelines that it is critical you deal with a true professional mortgage loan officer. This is not the time to work with someone new to the business, unless a supervisor is overseeing every step. Be sure to inquire about the level of experience your loan officer has. After all, this is the probably the biggest purchase in your life, so why not use the best?

(To use a do-it-yourself Pre-Qualification Form, which determines your ratios, make a copy of the following two-page form and use it as a guide.)

"Do Your Own Pre-Qual" Formula

The following formula allows you to pre-qualify yourself
within a reasonable amount of accuracy. This does not mean you absolutely
qualify—but it gives you a good starting point to see where you stand.

WHAT YOU WILL NEED:

- An online mortgage calculator (such as Google or other)
- A copy of your credit report or at a minimum, knowledge of your "middle credit score" (Example: Every mortgage credit report shows three scores, such as 680, 690, and 700. In this example, the middle score is 690.)
- Knowledge of monthly payments for all installment loans (cars, student, etc.) and all revolving credit (credit cards)
- A W-2, to calculate your gross monthly earnings
- Knowledge of the taxes on properties located in the area where you are looking to buy
- A general knowledge of how much home owner's insurance costs in your area
- Knowledge of any Homeowner's Association (HOA) fee tied to the property

You will also need to know the sales price and required loan amount before filling out the worksheets that follow.

Sales Price _____   Loan Amount _____

1. Multiply the sales price by the amount of your down payment (5%, 10%, 20%, etc.), then subtract that amount from the sales price to get your loan amount.

    Example: Sales price of $100,000 x 3.5% down payment = $3,500
    Down payment of $3,500 – $100,000 = loan amount of $96,500

2. Check your local lending rates and use an online mortgage calculator to determine your monthly payments for the loan amount.

PRE-QUALIFICATION CALCULATION – PART 1:

1. GROSS MONTHLY INCOME _____

2. MORTGAGE PAYMENT FROM ONLINE CALCULATOR _____

3. TAXES, INSURANCE AND HOA FEES (IF ANY) _____

4. ADD LINES 2 AND 3 _____

5. DIVIDE LINE 4 BY LINE 1 _____%
   This is your <u>housing/front ratio</u> and should not be higher than 38%

PRE-QUALIFICATION CALCULATION – PART 2:

1. GROSS MONTHLY INCOME _____

2. INSERT THE TOTAL FROM PART 1, LINE 4 _____

3. INSERT THE TOTAL OF ALL MONTHLY PAYMENTS FOR DEBTS,
   SUCH AS AUTO LOANS, CREDIT CARDS, STUDENT LOANS, ETC. _____

4. ADD LINES 2, 3 AND 4 _____

5. DIVIDE LINE 5 BY LINE 1 _____%
   This is your <u>back ratio</u> and should not be higher than 45%
   NOTE: This is due to change to a lower percentage of 43% in 2014.

ANALYSIS:

If the number on line 5 in Part 1 is 38% or less, you qualify for Part 1 of the prequalification. If it's over that amount, you may still qualify but you should consult a mortgage professional.

If the number on line 5 in Part 2 is 45% or less, you qualify for Part 2 of the prequalification. If it's over that amount, you may still qualify but you should consult a mortgage professional.

The reason is that conventional loans (Fannie Mae and Freddie Mac) allow up to 45% of gross monthly income for Part 2, while FHA allows up to 50%.

To make matters a bit more complicated, certain loans, such as VA and USDA, use even lower ratios. In addition, if you are putting down less than 20% on a loan, you will need to calculate in private mortgage insurance. Consult a mortgage professional for an exact monthly payment.

This form should not be misconstrued in any way shape or form as a final qualification.

CHAPTER 16

Credit Scores– The Achilles' Heel to Buyers

There are numerous parts to the pre-approval, and for that matter any loan approval. Of all the variables, credit scores are the most talked about—and rightly so, as they are the core benchmark used by lenders. In today's market, 640 has become the standard score for any loan; however, this is not hard and fast. Certain lenders will go to 620 for FHA loans and some want 660 for Conventional. The standard to keep in mind is 640.

Credit scores can in fact be raised using the proper tools and by working with regulated entities such as a credit bureau. Some bureaus offer analyzers, which tell the borrower what debts need to be paid down or paid off. The bottom line here is to begin correcting your credit profile long before applying for a loan. If you know you have not paid on time, you can be assured your credit will not pass the test for approval. Monitoring your credit is the best possible way to get a handle on where you stand and where you need to go.

Ask for a free credit report; you are entitled to one free report each year. Call any of the three bureaus to get your free report: TransUnion, Equifax or Experian.

WARNING: There are many entities out there that want you to believe that for hundreds or thousands of dollars they can repair your credit. In 99.99% of the time, they cannot—and will in fact only make it worse. Work with your lender. They know best the ways to help you reduce debt and/or maximize your scores.

If you have been able to show the proper income, credit score and documentation, you are ready to move forward with a loan application.

CHAPTER 17

Closing Costs

Closing costs are represented in two or three different forms. They are presented during pre-approval as a closing cost estimate worksheet. (See sample at the end of this chapter.) They are then presented at official application, per regulations on a form known as the "Good Faith Estimate," commonly referred to as the "GFE." (See Sample GFE at the end of this chapter.)

The last form a buyer and seller will see is the HUD-1. Both the HUD-1 Settlement Statement and the GFE are now designed to mirror each other, with the exception of including costs and credits such as real estate commissions, seller credits for utilities or other details specific to your loan.

Closing costs are one of the most unexpected and least considered factors among first-time homebuyers. On the other hand, those who have purchased before know that this is one of the core issues for deciding on a lender and what is needed to begin the home buying process.

UPDATE: Due to new Real Estate Settlement Procedures Act (RESPA) regulations, varying closing costs among lenders is much less an issue than it once was, due to guidelines and penalties that now protect borrowers from being gouged or overcharged (as many were during the boom years).

During the housing boom, many buyers would arrive at the closing table to find their closing costs had risen substantially; they had little or no choice to do anything but close the deal, as doing otherwise would mean breaking the contract and losing their deposit. This practice was carried out by unscrupulous loan officers and lenders who violated laws that were in place, although those laws were toothless and unenforced at the time. Of all the new regulations, this disclosure may be one of the rules that actually helps buyers.

As stated above, there are two types of closing cost estimates today: "actual" closing costs and "estimated" closing costs, depending on where you are in the process. If you are in the pre-approval mode you can request an estimate of fees, but this will be exactly that: an estimate. For a more accurate estimate, the lender must have all variables in order to calculate closing costs properly. This includes all financial information, a viable contract, the taxes and insurance on the property and whether any seller-paid closing costs are involved.

Today's environment has eliminated the issue of gouging, as lenders are now forced to be more competitive with their costs. The most important aspect of the new rules is that certain costs are fixed and cannot change at closing. These items include lender's points, charges for processing, underwriting and other fees. Today, borrowers pay charges as shown exactly by the lender and not a penny more.

Costs are provided to all borrowers who have a contract in place through the GFE. Again, lenders today use other forms of estimates in addition to the GFE for ease of reading and understanding of the potential costs during pre-approval, and even during full application.

Of critical importance for the buyer is to recognize that when asking for the lender's closing costs for the sake of comparison-shopping, be certain to compare apples to apples. For example, if you receive one estimate that only includes lender's closing costs while the other includes lender's costs plus title, insurance or survey costs, taxes, etc., you cannot make an informed decision.

Another problem here is the terminology. Some lenders may use a term like "doc prep fee," while others use "application fee." You must ask what the terms apply to. Most common today are the processing fee, underwriting fee, appraisal fee and credit fee. All other costs are for state taxes, closing and title work, escrows and interest.

Closing costs are those costs associated with the actual closing of the transaction. Closing costs include:

1. Lender's fees (processing and underwriting)

2. Appraisal and credit

3. Title fees

4. Escrows for taxes and insurance

5. State taxes and fees

6. Surveys

7. Pest tests

8. Prepaid interest

Closing costs can be estimated by your loan officer prior to your finding a property. However, due to the new regulations, once a property is inserted into the loan system, closing costs are considered a final estimate; if certain fees change, penalties will be imposed on the lenders.

The following list explains each cost in the order you will see it on the form:

1. Origination Points

Known as "Loan Origination" fees or more simply "points," these are charged by the lender for costs of the proposed mortgage loan. Origination fees (or points) are quoted as a percentage of the loan amount. One point is equal to 1% of the loan amount. In some cases, such as an FHA 203K loan, a point is added to cover the cost of the loan to the lender since there is much more risk involved in this type of loan.

2. Discount Points

Using the same explanation as above, discount points are quoted the same way. Discount points represent additional money you or the seller pay toward lowering the rate. One discount point is equal to 1% of the loan amount. In some cases, when there are "seller-paid" closing costs and after paying certain closing costs monies are left over, these funds may be applied to lower the rate.

To give you an idea of how much each point you pay to lower your rate equates to in savings, consider the following: Each point you pay for a 30-year loan reduces the rate between one-eighth (or .125) and one-quarter (.25) of a percentage point.

My personal opinion is you never pay points... unless you are a long-term buyer.

Following is a simple calculation to help determine whether or not you should pay points:

> Let's say your loan is for $150,000. The loan is a 30-year fixed rate term. This will be your primary home, but only for about three to four years, as maybe your job requires frequent moves. The cost of one point is 1%: 1% x $150k = $1,500
>
> *Option 1:*
>
> At a rate of 4.25% with no points, the monthly payment would be $1,254.

Option 2:

At a lower rate of 4% with one point, the monthly payment would be $1,217—for a savings of $37 per month.

To see if Option 2 (paying one point) is worth the time for a three- to four-year time period, subtract the difference between the payment with one point ($1,217) from the payment with no points ($1,254), which is $37 per month. Divide the cost of the point ($1,500) by the monthly savings ($37): 1500/37 = 41 (rounded). As you can see, it will take 41 months, or nearly three and a half years, to recoup the cost of the point.

In month 42, you will begin to see the benefits of paying the point—but that's nearly three and a half years. However, let's assume you are in the home for 10 years or more. Simply multiply the $37 per month times 120 months minus the cost of the point, and you will see you can save $2,940 over the 10 years: 120 x $37 = $4,440 - $1,500 = $2,940

This example illustrates how minimal an impact paying points makes, unless you plan to live in your home long-term.

3. Application Fee

Most lenders do not charge an application fee—or when they do, it includes the appraisal and credit report. This varies by state and lender so you must do your research to conclude what is the acceptable standard in your area.

4. Appraisal Fee

Not to be confused with the inspection fee, an appraisal is required on nearly all loans made in the US to determine the actual value of the property. The appraisal is also used to identify problems with the property such as roofs needing replacement or other functional issues of the home. Depending on the loan type, an appraisal may not be necessary. For example, on a Fannie Mae-foreclosed home, no appraisal is required if it is labeled as part of the Fannie Mae special financing program called HomePath (www.homepath.com). Other cases, such as with VA or FHA refinances, may also not require an appraisal. However, due to concerns with increased defaults, lenders are moving away from non-appraisal deals.

5. Credit Report Fee

This is one fee all lenders require. Credit reports identify qualified borrowers from a creditor's standpoint. Mentioned earlier, lenders rely upon three major national credit bureaus for their reports: Equifax, TransUnion and Experian. However, most lenders do not go directly to the three, but rather use private firms, which provide the required report as well as services to help lenders with the borrower's report. Consumers typically pay $15 to $55 for a report, which shows up on the closing statement.

6. Per Diem Interest

This is not a fee; it is a partial amount of your new monthly payment that is owed upon signing for a new home. For example, if the loan is closed and the money disbursed on December 15, the lender collects the interest on the loan as if it closed on January 1, with the first payment due February 1. Since the borrower received the loan on December 15, the lender expects to be paid interest for the period between December 15 and January 1. Therefore, the per diem charge for the interest is 15 days.

7. Settlement or Closing Fees

The lender requires a licensed and regulated closing firm—either an attorney or title company—to close the loan for the borrower. For doing the work, a "settlement" fee or "closing" fee is charged. The title business, meaning title companies who perform closings, has become very competitive; therefore a borrower should not be pushed into using a certain title company or attorney as it is illegal for anyone to require the use of a certain firm.

Also, it's important to note that not all states use title companies. Most of the New England states (MA, CT and NY) use attorneys. Attorneys go all out in preventing title companies from getting a foothold, as they are usually less expensive. However, since the downturn, attorneys have become much more competitive and so remain a cost-effective option.

8. Owner's and Lender's Title Insurance

In real estate, there are two types of title insurance policies: an owner's policy and a lender's policy. Just as lenders require fire insurance and other types of insurance coverage to protect their investments, nearly all institutional lenders require title insurance to protect the collateral secured by real estate. This is called "Lender's Title Insurance."

"Owner's Title Insurance" is mandatory on all purchases but not for refinances. In my opinion, it should be purchased—and is on 99% of all properties. For a small cost, Owner's Title Insurance gives buyers the peace of mind that no one will come knocking on their door to say, "Give me the keys because my great, great, great, great grandmother owned this home back in 1789!"

Title insurance companies research the history of the property in order to discover any possible disputes prior to the closing of the transaction. In the event a problem does exist, the buyer is alerted and has the option to walk away from the transaction, or work with the seller to resolve the issue. If the title insurance company found no problems in its search, or problems were found and resolved, a "Title Insurance Policy" or a "Policy with Exceptions" may be issued. This policy protects either the lender or owner (depending on the type of policy) against any future claims on the title of this property. In the event that a viable challenge to the title comes to light after the transaction, the title insurance company will protect the insured party against any losses.

9. Recording Fees

All states require the documentation of a loan to be recorded. The fees are based upon the number of pages and typically range between $200 and $300.

10. Escrows

Most loans today require that the borrower pay taxes and insurance along with their monthly principal and interest payments. In doing so, the bank is in essence setting up a reserve account, which collects enough funds to pay the subsequent year's taxes and insurance. To determine the amount of this ongoing payment, lenders calculate the number of months and collect the funds at closing, thereby ensuring there will be enough funds in the escrow accounts to pay the following year's renewals.

11. Deed Stamps, Tax Stamps, Transfer Tax, etc.

Every state collects taxes on real estate. Each refers to the fee in a different way and each collects taxes under different scenarios. (Florida is one of the worst, as it has three taxes.) These fees are based on a percentage of the loan amount, the sale price or a combination of both.

12. Ancillary Fees

Lenders today disclose all fees associated with the loan transaction, even those not their own. The purpose is to ensure that borrowers know exactly what the lender expects of them with regard to closing costs in order to close the loan. These fees may include but are not limited to survey fee, Realtor fee, pest fee, inspection fee and others.

The Good Faith Estimate (GFE)

The Good Faith Estimate is the form that provides a borrower with a preview of the charges and fees to expect in the loan transaction. In today's new lending environment, regulators are continuing to tinker with ways to make the loan process and related documentation easier to understand. However, in this effort, they have been making matters worse for borrowers. One by-product of this endeavor is the new Good Faith Estimate form, which imposes tolerances upon lenders that in many circumstances are fair, but in others are unfair. The new form has recently gone under fire, as it is more complicated than the form it replaced.

Each section in the GFE now directly corresponds to a section of the HUD-1 (the standardized document that lists every expense involved in a real estate or refinance transaction, which is presented to the borrower during the closing process).

In the new GFE, a tolerance level is assigned to each section. There are three different tolerance levels:

1. 0% Tolerance

If at the closing, any item in the "0% Tolerance" category is higher on the corresponding section of the HUD-1 when compared to the original GFE, the lender is responsible for covering the difference. These are fees such as lender's points and origination fees, underwriting and processing fees and others.

2. 10% Tolerance

Unlike the 0% Tolerance category, these items are not compared individually to their corresponding section in the HUD-1. Instead, all items in the "10% Tolerance" category are summed up on the GFE and compared against the sums for items on the HUD-1. In the event that the HUD-1 shows a total higher than 10% of the total on the GFE, the lender is responsible for any expense in excess of the 10% increase. This means that any one item in the 10% Tolerance category can increase more than 10% from the GFE to the HUD-1 without penalty to the lender, as long as the sum of all the items does not increase more than 10%. These fees may include title costs and others.

3. No Tolerance

A few sections of the new GFE fall into the "No Tolerance" section. These quotes can change with no penalty to the lender.

NOTE: There are circumstances that allow lenders to change fees, such as a new loan amount or an increase in homeowner's insurance, taxes, flood insurance, etc.

Now that you know how a GFE works and understand the fees for closing a loan, be mindful that at the actual closing there could be more credits and charges when the closing agent calculates such items as taxes due or seller-paid closing costs. The most important part of this section is knowing about the potential fees. Do not enter into a loan transaction blindly. Recognize that in addition to the down payment there are many other fees. Some of these are up-front, whereas you will not see others until you're at the closing.

While changes to the GFE disclosure are overdue, and some of those changes are positive, the implementation of many of the changes has caused nothing but headaches for lenders and borrowers alike.

NOTE: At the time of this writing, the Consumer Financial Protection Bureau (CFPB) is creating a new GFE. You can review the new GFE at http://www.hud.gov/offices/hsg/rmra/res/gfestimate.pdf

Date Prepared: Loan Number:

Approximate Loan Cost Illustration

Loan Officer:
Email:
Phone Number: Branch Name:
NMLS Id: Branch Phone:
Product Type:

APPROXIMATE COST OF CLOSING FEES	
Appraisal Fee	$375.00
Credit Report Fee	$20.00
Loan Processing Fee	$595.00
Underwriting Fee	$495.00
Condo Certification Fee	$350.00
Settlement or Closing	$500.00
Lenders Title Insurance	$250.00
Owners Title Insurance	$825.00
Endorsements	$200.00
Recording Fee	$200.00
Documentary Stamps	$420.00
Survey Fee	$350.00
Total Approximate Cost of Closing Fees	**$4,580.00**
APPROXIMATE COST OF PREPAID INTEREST AND ESCROW/RESERVES	
Interest for 10 days @ $12.33 per day	$123.30
HO6 Insurance	$600.00
Hazard Insurance	$200.00
County Property Taxes	$600.00
Aggregate Adjustment	($200.00)
Total Approximate Cost of Prepaid Interest and Escrows	**$1,323.30**
Total Approximate Cost of Settlement Charges	**$5,903.30**

APPROXIMATE TOTAL OF FUNDS NEEDED TO CLOSE		APPROXIMATE TOTAL MONTHLY PAYMENT	
Purchase Price/Total Liens	$150,000.00	Interest Rate	3.750%
less Earnest Money/Credits	$0.00	APR	3.892%
less Total Loan Amount	$120,000.00	Maturity Term 360 mos	30 yrs
less Secondary Financing Amount	$0.00		
less Borrower's closing cost paid by Seller	$0.00	Principal & Interest (or Interest Only payment)	$555.74
plus Mortgage Insurance or Funding Fee	$0.00	Other Financing (P&I)	$0.00
plus Approximate Closing Fees Pd by Borrower	$4,580.00	Real Estate Taxes	$200.00
plus Approximate Pre-paid Items/Reserves	$1,323.30	Insurance	$100.08
less POC fees paid by Borrower	$0.00	Homeowners Association (if applicable)	$0.00
		Mortgage Insurance (if applicable)	$0.00
		Other	$0.00
Total Approximate Funds needed to close	**$35,903.30**	**Total Approximate Monthly Payment**	**$855.82**

Down Payment	$30,000.00	20.00%

This is an example of the charges you may incur to close a mortgage loan of this type. This is not a Good Faith Estimate of Closing Costs or a Truth-In-Lending Disclosure. Once you apply for a loan, by providing us all required application information including a property address, you will be given a binding Good Faith Estimate of Closing Costs and a Truth-In-Lending disclosure. This is not a rate lock. To lock the interest rate we must have a complete application with all supporting documents including a copy of the real estate contract and your express request to lock your rate and fees. This is not a commitment to lend. Restrictions Apply. This is not a pre-approval or pre-qualification. Closing and settlement costs, reserve deposits, interest rate and APR are subject to change. Equal housing lender.

Borrower: _____   Date _____

_____   Date _____

Good Faith Estimate (GFE)

U.S. DEPARTMENT OF HOUSING AND URBAN DEVELOPMENT

	Loan Number	
Name of Originator	Borrower	
Originator Address	Property Address	
Originator Phone Number		
Originator Email	Date of GFE	

Purpose

This GFE gives you an estimate of your settlement charges and loan terms if you are approved for this loan. For more information, see HUD's *Special Information Booklet* on settlement charges, your *Truth-In-Lending Disclosures*, and other consumer information at www.hud.gov/respa. If you decide you would like to proceed with this loan, contact us.

Shopping for your loan

Only you can shop for the best loan for you. Compare this GFE with other loan offers, so you can find the best loan. Use the shopping chart on page 3 to compare all the offers you receive.

Important dates

1. The interest rate for this GFE is available through 8/19/2012 4:14 pm. After this time, the interest rate, some of your Loan Origination Charges, and the monthly payment shown below can change until you lock your interest rate.
2. This estimate for all other settlement charges is available through 9/6/2012.
3. After you lock your interest rate, you must go to settlement within 30 days (your rate lock period) to receive the locked interest rate.
4. You must lock the interest rate at least N/A days before settlement.

Summary of your loan

Your initial loan amount is	$120,000.00
Your loan term is	30 years
Your initial interest rate is	3.750%
Your initial monthly amount owed for principal, interest, and any mortgage insurance is	$555.74
Can your interest rate rise?	☒No ☐Yes, it can rise to a maximum of . The first change will be in
Even if you make payments on time, can your loan balance rise?	☒No ☐Yes, it can rise to a maximum of
Even if you make payments on time, can your monthly amount owed for principal, interest, and any mortgage insurance rise?	☒No ☐Yes, the first increase can be in and the monthly amount owed can rise to . The maximum it can ever rise to is $$
Does your loan have a prepayment penalty?	☒No ☐Yes, your maximum prepayment penalty is $
Does your loan have a balloon payment?	☒No ☐Yes, you have a balloon payment of due in years

Escrow account Information

Some lenders require an escrow account to hold funds for paying property taxes or other property-related charges in addition to your monthly amount owed of $555.74.
Do we require you to have an escrow account for your loan?
☐ No, you do not have an escrow account. You must pay these charges directly when due.
☒ Yes, you have an escrow account. It may or may not cover all of these charges. Ask us.

Summary of your settlement charges

A	Your Adjusted Origination Charges *(See page 2)*	$1,440.00
B	Your Charges for All Other Settlement Services *(See page 2)*	$4,463.30
A + B	**Total Estimated Settlement Charges**	$5,903.30

SAMPLE

Loan Number:

Understanding your estimated settlement charges

Your Adjusted Origination Charges	
1. Our origination charge This charge is for getting this loan for you.	$1,440.00
2. Your credit or charge (points) for the specific interest rate chosen ☒ The credit or charge for the interest rate of 3.750% is included in "Our origination charge." (See item 1 above.) ☐ You receive a credit of $ _____ for this interest rate of _____%. This credit **reduces** your settlement charges. ☐ You pay a charge of $ _____ for this interest rate of _____%. This charge (points) **increases** your total settlement charges. The tradeoff table on page 3 shows that you can change your total settlement charges by choosing a different interest rate for this loan.	$0.00
A Your Adjusted Origination Charges	$1,440.00

Some of these charges can change at settlement. See the top of page 3 for more information.

Your Charges for All Other Settlement Services	
3. Required services that we select These charges are for services we require to complete your settlement. We will choose the providers of these services.	$395.00

Service	Charge
Appraisal Fee	$375.00
Credit Report Fee	$20.00

4. Title services and lender's title insurance This charge includes the services of a title agent, for example, and title insurance to protect the lender, if required.	$950.00
5. Owner's title insurance You may purchase an owner's title insurance policy to protect your interest in the property.	$825.00
6. Required services that you can shop for These charges are for other services that are required to complete your settlement. We can identify providers of these services or you can shop for them yourself. Our estimates for providing these services are below.	$350.00

Service	Charge
Survey Fee	$350.00
Homeowners Dues Reserves	$0.00

7. Government recording charges These charges are for state and local fees to record your loan and title documents.	$200.00
8. Transfer Taxes These charges are for state and local fees on mortgages and home sales.	$420.00
9. Initial deposit for your escrow account This charge is held in an escrow account to pay future recurring charges on your property and includes ☒ all property taxes, ☒ all insurance, and ☐ other	$600.00
10. Daily interest charges This charge is for the daily interest on your loan from the day of your settlement until the first day of the next month or the first day of your normal mortgage payment cycle. This amount is $12.33 per day for 10 days (if your settlement is).	$123.30
11. Homeowner's insurance This charge is for the insurance you must buy for the property to protect from a loss, such as fire.	$600.00

Policy	Charge
HO6 Insurance	$600.00

B Your Charges for All Other Settlement Services	$4,463.30
A + B **Total Estimated Settlement Charges**	$5,903.30

Good Faith Estimate (HUD-GFE) 2

SAMPLE

Instructions

Loan Number: _____

Understanding which charges can change at settlement

This GFE estimates your settlement charges. At your settlement, you will receive a HUD-1, a form that lists your actual costs. Compare the charges on the HUD-1 with the charges on this GFE. Charges can change if you select your own provider and do not use the companies we identify. (See below for details.)

These charges **cannot increase** at settlement	The total of these charges **can increase up to 10%** at settlement	These charges **can change** at settlement
• Our origination charge • Your credit or charge (points) for the specific interest rate chosen (*after you lock in your interest rate*) • Your adjusted origination charges (*after you lock in your interest rate*) • Transfer taxes	• Required services that we select • Title services and lender's title insurance (*if we select them or you use companies we identify*) • Owner's title insurance (*if you use companies we identify*) • Required services that you can shop for (*if you use companies we identify*) • Government recording charges	• Required services that you can shop for (*if you do not use companies we identify*) • Title services and lender's title insurance (*if you do not use companies we identify*) • Owner's title insurance (*if you do not use companies we identify*) • Initial deposit for your escrow account • Daily interest rate charges • Homeowner's insurance

Using the tradeoff table

In this GFE, we offered you this loan with a particular interest rate and estimated settlement charges. However:
• If you want to choose this same loan with **lower settlement charges**, then you will have a **higher interest rate**.
• If you want to choose this same loan with a **lower interest rate**, then you will have a **higher settlement charges**.
If you would like to choose an available option, you must ask us for this table. Please ask for additional information if the table is not completed.
Loan originators have the option to complete this table.

	The loan in this GFE	The same loan with lower settlement charges	The same loan with lower interest rate
Your initial loan amount	$ 120,000.00	$ 120,000.00	$ 120,000.00
Your initial interest rate [1]	3.750%	%	%
Your initial monthly amount owed	$ 555.74	$	$
Change in the monthly amount owed from this GFE	No change	You will pay $ **more** every month	You will pay $ **less** every month
Change in the amount you will pay at settlement with this interest rate	No change	Your settlement charges will be **reduced** by $	Your settlement charges will **increase** by $
How much your total estimated settlement charges will be	$ 5,903.30	$	$

[1] *For an adjustable rate loan, the comparisons above are for the initial interest rate before adjustments are made.*

Using the shopping chart

Use this chart to compare GFEs from different loan originators. Fill in the information by using a different column for each GFE you receive. By comparing loan offers, you can shop for the best loan.

	Loan 1	Loan 2	Loan 3	Loan 4
Loan originator name				
Initial loan amount	$120,000.00			
Loan term	30 years			
Initial interest rate	3.750%			
Initial monthly amount owed	$555.74			
Rate lock period				
Can interest rate rise?	No			
Can loan balance rise?	No			
Can monthly amount owed rise?	No			
Prepayment penalty?	No			
Balloon payment?	No			
Total Estimated Settlement Charges	$5,903.30			

If your loan is sold in the future

Some lenders may sell your loan after settlement. Any fees lenders receive in the future cannot change the loan you receive or the charges you paid at settlement.

CHAPTER 18

Loan Types

Now that we have you ready and able to move forward, the loan process truly begins in earnest. You will need all the items on the checklist provided by your lender, and you will be on the hot seat to deliver anything that is missing along the way to approval. You, the loan officer and the processor will make or break a successful loan approval. Always remember that no one knows you personally, and that anything you can do to help those on your team to understand your circumstances will expedite the process.

Our next step is to discuss program options.

Whether you are a first-time buyer or an experienced buyer, remember that the loan programs are constantly changing. In years gone by, we had No-Doc and Liar loans. We had Interest-Only and "2-Year ARMS." Very little was done with FHA, as everyone considered it cumbersome. Today is a new world; FHA is king for people who are buying any property that they will live in as their primary home.

The fact that we have had declining markets in many states (i.e., home values going down) has resulted in many buyers attempting to purchase primary homes by putting the least amount of money down (typically with an FHA loan at the rate of 3.5%). This was a wise choice, of course—who wants to throw money out the window while prices continued to drop (until recently). If you do the math on, say, a $100,000 purchase with 20% down ($20,000) and the home drops in value by 5%, the buyer just lost $5,000 of his hard-earned money and now only has 15% equity in the home.

Gone are the No-Doc and Liar loans, yet we still have Interest-Only loans. As its name implies, an Interest-Only loan simply means that there is no principal pay-down. The question is: Why do lenders continue to offer this product, when we have the lowest rates in history and we know Interest-Only loans have wreaked havoc on those who have ultimately lost their homes?

In reality, the Interest-Only program—like the No-Doc loans for self-employed people—make sense in some circumstances. For instance, if your company is relocating you and you know that in two to three years you may be moving again, the Interest-Only product would be a great option. Or if you are self-employed, have great credit and can put down 25% to 30%, the No-Doc loan, which was used frequently prior to the meltdown, was a great product and had a solid history with very few defaults.

The problem with the No-Doc loan is that the big guys got in the game. Instead of requiring 25% or more down, they went the other way by writing No-Docs with zero down and much lower credit scores. These are the types of lenders who are responsible for ruining an entire industry, and are putting unnecessary pressure on lenders who today are adhering to proper standards when it comes to underwriting. This is exactly why the pendulum has swung so far to the left from where it should be.

When used correctly, No-Doc had a very low default rate and helped the people it was supposed to: those who were self-employed and those who worked on commission. Unfortunately, when left to the greed of those who saw only fast profits, the program was used to scam lenders and buyers alike.

For the vast number of borrowers today, the choices are between two types of loans:

- Government loans, such as FHA, VA or USDA for primary homebuyers only

- FHA, VA and USDA loans for condos, only if the condo project is approved by one of the agencies

- Conventional loans, which typically fall under Fannie Mae or Freddie Mac, for all types of properties including second homes and investment. Fannie and Freddie also approve condos and will finance others not on the "approved" list.

We will discuss Non-Conventional loans for foreign nationals and Jumbo loan buyers later in the segment.

Government Loans

Government loans are defined as all loans that are backed up by the government as insurance to the lender. Government loans have various requirements including loan limits (usually by county), income restrictions for loans such as USDA, and ratio differences such as those required by VA and USDA versus FHA. Your loan officer can help you identify each variable that applies to you.

Conventional Loans

Conventional loans are primarily those issued under Fannie Mae and Freddie Mac guidelines. Conventional loans are currently limited to a loan amount on a national basis of $417,000 for single-family homes (including condos); $533,850 for two-unit home;

$645,300 for three-units; and $801,950 for four-units. Loan terms for Conventional come as 10-, 15-, 20- or 30-year loans.

Alaska, Guam, Hawaii and the US Virgin Islands also have specific loan limits of $625,500 for one-units, $800,725 for two-units, $967,950 for three-units and $1,202,925 for four-units. These amounts reflect the prices of homes in these areas.

NOTE: These loan amounts change annually.

There is one other group of Conventional loans called "High Cost Area" loans. You can go to the following website for all information on Fannie Mae at:

https://www.efanniemae.com/sf/refmaterials/loanlimits/

Specific Loan Types

FHA Straight Loans

The FHA "Straight" is a loan that is insured to the lenders by the government and requires just 3.5% down on an owner-occupied home only. The loan is structured a bit differently due to the government's attempt to recoup lost monies, as well as to insure the risk it is taking with the low down payment. The FHA Straight loan adds a monthly mortgage insurance payment of 1.25% of the loan amount. The payment calculation is as follows: $150,000 x 1.25% = $1,875/12 months = $156.25 monthly.

This loan also adds onto the actual loan amount with an "Up-Front Mortgage Insurance Premium" (UFMIP) charge of 1.75% of the loan amount. The calculation for this new loan amount is as follows: $150,000 x 1.75% = $2,625 + $150,000 = $152,625.

The advantages to an FHA loan include flexibility with credit, higher debt-to-income ratios and a low down payment of 3.5%. As an example, FHA will allow certain income scenarios that seem outside the box to Fannie Mae and other lenders in order to be considered approvable. An FHA loan can be used on a primary home only at this time.

FHA 203K Renovation Loans

Perhaps one of the best-kept secrets about loan programs is the FHA "203K Renovation" loan. This is the only loan (other than Fannie Mae's HomePath Renovation Mortgage and HomeStyle) that allows a buyer to purchase the home and simultaneously receive funds for renovation and/or repairs. Back in the day, a borrower could go to a local bank after purchasing his new home and request a construction or remodeling loan for fix-ups. This type of loan is rarely available. The HomePath Renovation Mortgage option also allows for 3% down to purchase and renovate a new home, although very few lenders are able to or want to participate in this program.

There are two versions of the FHA 203K Renovation loan:
1. Streamline 203K—The FHA 203K "Streamline" loan allows a buyer to find a home that needs repairs or simple cosmetic renovations such as new carpet, paint, kitchen, bath, etc. For example, a buyer can find a home for $150,000 that needs a new roof and kitchen; as long as the repairs do not exceed $35,000 (including 203K fees) the loan is classified as a Streamline.

NOTE: The Streamline does not allow for structural renovations, so be sure to go over the details with your 203K specialist.

You will want to work with someone who knows this program, as it is paper-intensive and requires someone extremely knowledgeable to set it up. Most lenders have well-trained and certified specialists on board, which you might check with your Realtor about. You may also log onto HUD's website to search for a 203K specialist: http://www.hud.gov/ll/code/llslcrit.cfm

2. Consultant 203K—The FHA 203K "Consultant" loan is similar to

the Streamline, but it provides for structural work and allows the borrower to go over the $35,000 limit for larger renovations.

NOTE: No luxury items can be included in a 203K loan. As an example, pools or cabanas are not allowed, with the exception of $1,500 for equipment repair or cleaning of a damaged pool.

For more on FHA 203K Renovation loans, visit: http://portal.hud.gov/hudportal/HUD?src=/program_offices/housing/sfh/203k/203kabou

Conventional Loans

These are Fannie Mae and Freddie Mac structured loans, which can be used to purchase primary homes, second homes and investment properties. The difference between Conventional and FHA is the down payment is larger (minimum 5% with mortgage insurance and up to 30% down required for an investment property). These ranges change and you will need to check with your lender for the newest limits. As an example, Florida homebuyers are required to put down 20% to 30% for a condo, depending on whether the property is a second home, primary or investment, whereas states that have been unaffected by the downturn will accept 5% to 10% down.

Fannie and Freddie also offer special Conventional loan programs such as HomePath, the financing package for Fannie Mae foreclosed homes. The program allows for no appraisal and only 3% down in most cases. Investors can put down as little as 15%, compared to 30% on a typical property that is not in foreclosure.

For more information about the HomePath program, visit: www.homepath.com

HomePath also offers a renovation program known as "Home-Style." Whereas HomePath is available only on Fannie Mae owned foreclosures, the HomeStyle loan is not property specific; it does not have to be owned by Fannie Mae. A HomeStyle loan allows a borrower to purchase a property that involves light to moderate renovation *plus* major structural renovations, additions, attic or basement build-outs.

NOTE: This is a program that very few lenders write. Most opt to switch a borrower to an FHA 203K Renovation loan.

For more information on Conventional loans, visit:
https://www.efanniemae.com/sf/mortgageproducts/pdf/hsreno-facts.pdf
http://www.homepath.com/incentives.html#improvedProperties

VA Loans
Another loan program that is widely missed by the public, and more specifically military veterans, is the VA loan. The program allows for 100% financing to any veteran and/or active military personnel, depending on the status of their eligibility certificate (found online).

For more information on VA loans, visit:
http://www.benefits.va.gov/homeloans/eligibility.asp

USDA Loans
Loans with the United States Department of Agriculture (USDA), Rural Housing, are another well-kept secret. The USDA allows lower income borrowers to purchase homes in designated parts of the country. The myth is that these homes are out in the boonies, but in fact many are situated in well-known metro areas.

If you find an eligible property and meet the income limits established by the USDA, this is a loan that allows for 100% financing!

To find out if a property is eligible and for more information on USDA loans, visit:
http://eligibility.sc.egov.usda.gov/eligibility/welcomeAction.do

State and County Bond Programs and Down Payment Assistance
Every state, and in fact many counties, have their own loan programs which can usually be found online. These programs can help those who do not have down payment monies or closing costs. The programs are typically used in tandem with an FHA, VA or USDA program, and the borrower will need to research each set of guidelines for the state they are in.

For more information on these programs, visit your state and county websites.

Non-Conventional Loans
Non-Conventional loans include loans for foreign nationals, Jumbo loans, "Wrap-Around Mortgages" and others. A wide variety of private lenders in today's market cater to niche buyers who cannot qualify for traditional FHA or Conventional loans. While these lenders are out there, buyers should check with a mortgage professional to see if they have the necessary relationships to offer such a program.

As an example, the hardest hit groups of borrowers are foreigners from countries like the United Kingdom, Brazil, Germany or others. There are lenders who will finance them, but the guidelines are unique and it is sometimes tough to fit that round peg into this particular square hole. Requirements for 50% down are not uncommon, and the loan types are nearly always adjustable rate loans. The reason for such strict requirements is that after the meltdown, the foreign buyers who jumped into the rush to buy left just as quickly by walking away from down payments of 5%, 10%, 15% and even 20%. Lenders today tend to go after the more affluent foreign buyers.

Jumbo borrowers have many more options, as the large banks and most lenders offer Jumbo loans up to $1 million. However, once above this threshold, the choices become more difficult as the limits and options for financing decrease. Again, checking with your lender to see if they have relationships outside their traditional programs will help. This scenario is not uncommon, but it requires research.

CHAPTER 19

Property Types—
The Landscape Has Changed!

Ten years ago there would have been no need to address the issue of property types. Today we have numerous types of new properties due to the housing crisis. Some of these properties cause the borrower unexpected frustration, and in some cases a loss of monies if not well informed.

Today's market includes short sales, foreclosures (REOs), auctions and many damaged properties due to unhappy owners who have been forced into foreclosure. Due to the foreclosure issues, there are very little direct seller/owner-to-buyer scenarios in certain markets. In many states, transactions are mostly bank-owned properties sold by the bank direct to the buyer—and because of that, rarely do we see a smooth transaction. Therefore, the following should be useful in your search.

REOs and Short Sales

REOs and short sales are two unique types of properties. I could write an entire book on just these two; however, for our immediate informational needs, I would simply caution buyers to be prepared for a non-traditional process.

Short Sales

A short sale appears to be the tougher of the two types. A buyer MUST keep in mind that just because there is an agreement in writing with the property's owner(s), it does NOT mean you have a deal. It is not the property owner's (seller's) agreement that counts—it's the seller's bank, and before an answer may be given to a buyer, the bank will put the seller through major hurdles in order to identify whether they qualify and are approved for the short sale. Sellers of short sales must submit substantial paperwork to the bank, along with a property evaluation by the listing Realtor, to allow the bank to make an informed decision. The bank and NOT the seller sets the final price.

Buying a short sale property becomes even more difficult when the seller has more than one mortgage. During the hay day, many buyers obtained what is known as "piggyback" loans, meaning they held both a first mortgage and a second mortgage in order to avoid paying private mortgage insurance. (Anything less than 20% down requires a monthly payment of mortgage insurance, which protects the bank.) Now, the buyer has to negotiate with two banks versus one—and this scenario becomes very difficult, since the first mortgage lender could give two rat's behinds as to what happens to the second mortgage holder's position.

These types of sales can take from 30 days to (in drastic cases) a year. As we sit here today, the government is considering a rule to impose new guidelines on these types of sales and force the banks into adhering to no longer than a 75-day turnaround.

REOs (Real Estate Owned)

When purchasing an REO home, you will want to be sure you are working with an REO specialist, as again, the banks are playing hardball.

The first thing a buyer needs to know is that the REO properties owned by the banks are distributed to asset managers who manage the sales of these homes through a network of accredited Realtors. Asset managers create relationships with the designated listing Realtors and work in tandem to move the homes. The chosen Realtors have control over these properties and all offers go through them exclusively. The paperwork is extensive when compared to a traditional sale, and there can be fierce competition to purchase one of these homes. The competition among agents to become approved for REO sales is just as brutal—and that would be putting it mildly.

The asset manager's job is to liquidate the property at the highest price. Depending on the property's condition and price, a bidding war could occur. In many cases, when these properties come online for sale, the asset managers give first-time homebuyers a two-week head start. These head starts are specific only to Fannie Mae, Freddie Mac and HUD borrowers. They can be found online at websites such as www.homepath.com (Fannie Mae's website for foreclosures) as well as on the HUD.gov homepage for Government loans. The head starts are not overtly advertised, so you need to ask the listing Realtors for more information.

REOs can become nerve-wracking, and this is where you must be careful with your offer as well as the selling party's acceptance. Typically, the banks want a quick turnaround, knowing full well this will not happen in today's market unless the buyer has been proactive in getting approved. The key to a happily-ever-after REO story is to get a full pre-approval, if possible.

NOTE: Every REO contract contains a penalty clause for the possibility of failing to close on time. You may get one reprieve from missing the closing date, but after *one miss—and unless the miss is due to the lender's fault—the game is on and you had best close on time!*

The following two websites are great resources for learning more about short sales and REOs:

Fannie Mae properties: <u>www.homepath.com</u>

Freddie Mac properties: <u>www.homesteps.com</u>

Again, if the property you are trying to purchase is not being properly handled by competent agents, you will be about to begin your worst nightmare. There are not enough words to describe the chaos these types of transactions can cause. Be sure that you do not find yourself in the middle of either a short sale or REO and working with incompetent agents.

Condominium

Once the darling of real estate and positioned as a solid choice for retirees as second homes and investment, these properties are now by far the toughest to finance due to the glut that exists throughout US markets such as Florida, Arizona, Nevada and other condo-convenient areas floundering due to the housing crisis.

When people walk away from a condo, the consequences are devastating, as the owners remaining in the community now must find a way to make up the lost revenues from the monthly dues. This can lead to legal issues, which only make it worse for someone to buy—for example, Fannie Mae will not finance a unit under pending litigation.

Other issues include requirements by Fannie Mae and Freddie Mac that put specific guidelines in place for the association to meet in order for a loan to be issued on a condo. Guidelines for these issues include questions such as:

- How many people rent?

- Is there a rental office on the premises?
- Is the property a condo-hotel (a trend, back in the day)?
- Is there enough cash in the reserves of the budget?

And much more! When a buyer purchases a condo, it becomes a two-step process. First, the condo association and then the buyer must be approved. All lenders use a "declined list," which is kept on condos that are in trouble. If a buyer finds a property on that list, he will be told that the loan cannot be done on that particular project.

To check if a condo is approved by HUD (for FHA, VA or USDA loans), go to:
https://entp.hud.gov/idapp/html/condlook.cfm

To check Fannie Mae-approved condos, go to:
https://www.efanniemae.com/sf/refmaterials/approvedprojects/

Those who have cash do well by purchasing at extremely low prices. However, they do run some risk if the condo association is in any danger with regard to its financial position.

Primary Home vs. Secondary vs. Investor

In today's world, "primary" means an owner-occupied home—not renting and not using the property for a second home or an investment. A "secondary" is a second home or a home that is used for nothing more than a vacation home. And an "investor" is an investment property—a property with which the buyer intends to rent or lease for a profit.

Buyers of primary and secondary homes receive the best rates and terms. For example, an individual buying a primary home today could obtain a rate of 3.875% to 4%, while an investment property would require a rate of nearly 5%. In addition, a down payment for a primary residence could range from 0% for VA, 3.5% for FHA and 0% for USDA. If you notice, all Government loans are primary owner-occupied only. Borrowers purchasing a primary residence with 5% or more down can also use Conventional loans from Fannie Mae or Freddie Mac.

Second homes require higher down payments, depending on the region. In Florida, for instance, a second home requires a minimum of 10% down; during the era of the real estate crash, this was as high as 20%.

Investment homes are another story, as they require anywhere from 25% to 30% down.

Understanding the differences among rates and how much down payments can vary simply by the type of home being purchased has brought the flippers into the housing markets. In the past, before the housing crash, many buyers who fancied themselves savvy buyers actually thought they had outsmarted the banks by saying they were purchasing a primary or second home when in actuality, they knew they were going to move in for a very short period of time then leave and turn the property into a rental. They were able to achieve their goals without many questions or quality control from lenders.

Today is a different time and a whole new world of regulation. Those buyers who purchased an investment property they called a primary home may have thought that going with a smaller down payment meant nothing other than alleviating a drain on their cash in the bank, but they were actually committing fraud; those borrowers are now being pursued for the crime. Today, if a buyer attempts to purchase a primary residence with the intent to use it as an investment property, they will be surprised by the stringent guidelines that are now in place to assure the lender that the property will be used as a primary or second home, and not investment. Today's lenders have entire quality control units whose sole job is to review documentation and trace any borrower who fits the profile for purchasing a primary home for the purpose of renting.

CHAPTER 20

Bankruptcies, Foreclosures, Short Sales, Loan Modifications... How Do They Affect Your Future and Buying a Home?

One of the most frequently asked questions a lender receives is primarily due to the housing meltdown: "Since I lost my home through foreclosure (or bankruptcy, or short sale, or even loan modification), when will I be able to purchase another home?"

In the beginning of this book, we identified who makes the rules. The rules for who can buy a home after a bankruptcy or foreclosure is one of those on which all of those entities have had a say. Below you will find a recently updated chart of what the new guidelines say for each category with regard to when a tarnished buyer may qualify for another home purchase loan.

While the guidelines state you may be eligible, you must understand that credit will continue to be one of the largest factors. As an example, three years after a bankruptcy, you may be eligible to purchase a home; however, this is not a carte blanche ticket to eligibility, as the guidelines go deeper. They require that you must show that you have rebuilt your credit, and that you have opened a number of new trade lines. In other words, the guidelines are just that: a guide for an underwriter to go by. It's still up to the borrowers to show that they have changed their spending and saving patterns.

You may also qualify for hardships, but this does not include the obvious, such as "I lost my job," or "We got divorced." Hardship exceptions are for true hardships, such as medical or disability. The clause below is taken from the FHA guidelines and provides some clarity: *Extenuating circumstances are created by non-recurring events that are beyond the borrower's control such as extended illness, loss of a job due to corporate downsizing or layoffs or the death of a spouse. These events often result in a sudden, significant, and prolonged reduction in income or a catastrophic increase in financial obligations.*

(See the Bankruptcy/Foreclosure/Short Sale/Loan Modification Grid at the end of Chapter 14.)

CHAPTER 21

Rates vs. Service

While most borrowers will tell you they want the lowest rate, their position changes dramatically when they are faced with lenders who:

- Drag their feet during processing
- Don't return calls
- Cause the borrower to lose their deposit or even a great rate that was locked
- Lose the deal completely

Times have changed and borrowers who do their homework know that losing one-eighth of a percentage in rate is not worth losing the deal or a deposit. No one wants to wait 90 days to close a loan that should take 30 days or less. Therefore, the following is only a recommendation. This guide grades lenders based on actual experiences within the market.

Nothing that is printed here should be used as a basis for your final decision; it is simply a guide to help you research the lenders in your area. As a borrower, you need to ask friends, co-workers, Realtors and title companies who they believe is the best performer in your market. Doing your homework is the answer.

Service grades

The following grades are the subjective opinion of the author only.

Large Box Banks	D	You are a number among millions and service is not a number one priority (even though they tell you every day that they are the best in TV and Internet ads).
Regional Banks	C	Some do well, but they are just one step below the large banks and you are again a number among thousands.
Community Banks	B	Most do well, as they are smaller than the large banks and focus a bit more on service.
Independents	B	Most do well, again being smaller than large banks; furthermore, they only offer mortgages versus checking/savings and other financial services. However, be certain to research their back office (processing and underwriting).
Mortgage Brokers	B	Most do well, but again, do the research. While they too only focus on mortgages, some are too small and cannot handle large numbers of clients. Seek referrals.

Notice that no lender receives an A. This is due to the many moving parts of lending. No lender has figured out how to streamline the process and in fact will never be able to do so with the current abundance of ongoing regulations and immense pressure to avoid the repurchase of any loans.

The most significant difference between banks and private independent lenders is that banks focus on more than just mortgages, whereas independents and mortgage brokers focus solely on home loans. In fact, most banks only offer mortgages as a path to cross-selling more products, which are typically more profitable. They believe the one-stop shopping aspect is attractive, and therefore push their mortgage loan officers to sell (for referral fees) all products—not just mortgages.

The independents and brokers will argue that incentivizing bank loan officers to sell many other products in effect dilutes their knowledge, implying that private lenders offer the more informed choice.

Bottom line: Do you research, get referrals, and go with the lender that best suits your needs.

If you're talking with a mortgage banker or mortgage broker, you only need go to the Nationwide Mortgage Licensing System & Registry (NMLS) (http://www.nmlsconsumeraccess.org) and search for the individual's name. You can also call the better Business Bureau and check with your local Chamber of Commerce.

CHAPTER 22

Pitfalls Borrowers Must Prepare For

No one ever wants to hear "gotcha!" when in the middle of a loan process, or for that matter, in anything we do in life. Below are the most common pitfalls or "gotchas" in mortgage lending; I believe there are plenty more where these originated from, as guidelines and rules are changing daily. Your loan officers today are at the mercy of the gang at the top who makes the rules, BUT they can help you avoid the pitfalls below.

Here are just a few of those "gotchas:"

1. Inquiries on Your Credit Report

Every time you consider making an acquisition and the creditor obtains a credit report, it's reported on your credit report as an inquiry. When you apply for a mortgage, those inquiries must be justified in a formal letter of explanation or the lender may provide you with a form that you can complete. If you did take on new credit, the lender wants to know the terms and conditions or if there is a new payment that they cannot see on the credit report. If you were just shopping—even with another lender—you must explain.

2. Large Deposits on Bank Statements

This is one of the most disrupting "gotchas" of all the items listed here. Any time there is an "out of the ordinary" deposit on a bank statement—which you provide—the lender will want to know exactly where the money came from. The requirement states that the borrower must provide documentation and a "complete sourcing" of the monies deposited. If the monies cannot be sourced, the amounts will be left out—jeopardizing the availability of funds needed for down payments and/or deposits. Be prepared for this and document all deposits. Lenders have no issues with deposits such as employment direct deposit, social security or pension income, but it's the odd deposits they want to know about.

The reason: So-called "mattress money" does not work when applying for a mortgage—all deposits must be identified. The government is constantly on the lookout for monies coming into the country illegally; there is also a big issue today with money laundering between gangs and foreign networks, including terrorists.

3. Gifts From Family Members

Any time a family member provides a gift, a gift letter provided by the lender must be completed. The donor must show that the funds were available at the time the gift was made, in most cases by simply showing a bank statement; and the borrower must be able to show the deposit into their account. Gifts can also be wired at the time of closing, but this is not the preferred method, as it also must be sourced thoroughly by the lender.

4. Identity of Interest

An "Identity of Interest," or "Non-Arm's Length" transaction occurs when a personal or business relationship exists between the borrower and the builder, seller or lender. These transactions pose an increased risk for fraud and additional precautions must be taken in order for the lender to evaluate and prudently underwrite that risk. In-depth analysis of transactions between parties with family or business relationships may reveal unsupported values, straw borrowers, Non-Arm's Length or "At-Interest" influences, inflated sales prices, or excessive fees or disbursements.

These transactions include:

- Family sales or transfers
- Corporate sales or transfers
- Mortgagors employed in the real estate or construction trades who are involved in the construction, financing or sale of the subject property
- Some transactions involving principals, a lender or other vendor (such as an appraiser, settlement agent, title company, etc.) who is involved in the lending process for the subject property

Note: The examples given here do not represent all types of Identity of Interest transactions. Different relationships within a transaction may require more prudent underwriting review and additional underwriting requirements.

These transactions involve persons who are not closely tied or related, but who may have a greater vested interest in the transaction—such as a party who plays more than one role in the same transaction (selling/listing agent and mortgage broker, for example). At-Interest transactions carry increased risk due to the greater vested interest in the transaction by one of the parties.

An "Arm's Length" transaction is one in which the parties are dealing from equal bargaining positions, with neither party being subject to the control or dominant influence of the other. The transaction must be treated with fairness, integrity and legality. Generally, Arm's Length transactions are used to establish fair market values for sales transactions.

All Non-Arm's Length transactions are considered At-Interest transactions; however, At-Interest transactions are not always Non-Arm's Length transactions. Examples of At-Interest transactions include:

- Builder also acting as Realtor/broker
- Realtor/broker selling own property
- Realtor/broker acting as the listing/seller agent as well as the mortgage broker

The following transactions are usually considered "Arm's Length," even though they are between family members:

- Spousal buyout due to divorce
- Interest buyout of an inherited property
- Gift of a down payment—when the source is the family member's equity in the sale of the subject property

Specific Non-Arm's Length and At-Interest transactions include:

- Family Sales: This is a transaction where one family member is selling to another. Often there is no real estate agent involved or the agent may also be a family member. These transactions carry the potential for increased risk because they may in fact be bailout situations (e.g., the selling party has financial problems and is unable to refinance on his or her own, and a family member takes on the risk).
- Gift of Equity: Gift equity in a subject property is an acceptable source of down payment, as long as the amount of equity has been verified. The donor must provide a gift letter. Borrowers must invest 5% of their own funds for loan-to-value ratios greater than 80%.
- Employer/Employee Sales: In this type of transaction, a

building or development company may sell a property to an employee who does not hold a principal ownership interest in the building or developing company.

5. Buying a Flipped Property

This became a new issue for lenders as the investment community realized they could buy homes cheap, fix them up and sell for a significant profit. There are specific rules for buying one of these types of properties, and the guidelines should be carefully reviewed with your loan officer.

6. Buy and Bail

This newest scam being played upon lenders makes it difficult for those buyers who are legitimately attempting to buy a new property while owning another property in the same state. If the property that the borrower currently owns is under water (i.e., the borrower owes more than the home is worth), the borrower will need a very strong reason for the move to the new home.

The definition of the buy-and-bail scam is: Savvy homeowners of properties who owed more than the properties were worth and figured out a way to walk away and still own a home. The game was actually simple. The owner would find a new home that was selling for much less than the home they currently owned, and apply for financing. Upon buying the new home, they would wait six months or longer and then walk away from the old home. Lenders finally caught on around 2010. Now, thanks to a few of those scammers, legitimate borrowers who truly need to move are put through their paces as they attempt to buy for reasons such as downsizing or job opportunity. Once again, we see how the few bad apples have ruined a legitimate business so that now, everyone pays.

CHAPTER 23

Understanding the Real Estate Contract

Part of your learning experience with this book is to know what you are signing! Putting an offer on a new property is just one step of the contract process. Once the offer is accepted, the true process begins.

Remember, consider all options before making your offer, as this is a contract that will lock you in for a long period of time. Be sure your Realtor is experienced and has made all attempts to make an offer with your goals in mind. If seller concessions (such as paying some of the closing costs) are available, be sure you have discussed this before signing the contract.

Once the offer is accepted, the contract will be drawn up to state exactly what will be expected from all parties. There are certain sections you'll want to pay close attention to. I describe below, using a Florida sales and purchase contract, the key sections of a typical contract. You will want to review a standard contract in your state in order to understand the various sections. The best source for such research is your Realtor or the Association of Realtors in your county or area. For more information, visit www.realtor.org.

The Real Estate Contract

Following are the pertinent sections to pay special attention to: Sections 1, 2, 3, 4, 5, 7, and 9.

Section 1 is typically for the names of the buyers and sellers and the address of the property. It may depend on your state, but the contract may also provide a section for the buyers and sellers to list items that are staying with the house, such as appliances.

Section 2 is where the sales price and the amount of the deposit you have agreed to put down are shown. Your deposit may be as low as 1% or as high as 10% of your offer. This amount typically varies, as this is an offer and not a final deal so you can put down a minimal number. However, if you are in a situation where you have put a previous deposit on an offer, the sellers will want to see the balance of that particular deposit, which is known as "earnest money." As an example, you make an offer with a $1,000 deposit, but the true deposit upon acceptance requires $10,000; you must make up this difference immediately upon acceptance of your offer.

There is a line within the same area of Section 2 asking for a date when the balance of the deposit will be due. You can insert a date that allows time for a second look, or inspection. Typically, you will be required to put down the balance of the required deposit (1% to 10%) within a very short period of time.

Section 3 is for those offers that are still not accepted. This section is used during the negotiation process, as by that time you will have a deposit in place. Once your offer is accepted, you will most likely be asked to deposit the balance of the required amount.

Section 4 is the most critical. This is the area that states the closing date. Most Realtors and sellers will push for 30 days to close, which in today's environment is doable but leaves no room for unexpected problems. The standard is 45 days. If you find yourself being pushed into 30 days, push back. The exception to this rule is when a buyer is using a renovation loan, such as the FHA 203K program, which will require 60 days for closing.

Section 5 is for extensions needed when the lender cannot provide funds due to a regulatory issue. The other purpose for extensions revolves around weather. The term used to describe events that are unavoidable in a real estate contract is force majeure.

Section 7 is the next critical section of the contract. This section identifies the type of financing that will be obtained and the amount that is being borrowed or specifies that the buyer is paying cash. The key portions of this clause have to do with non-cash buyers.

NOTE: Any time there is a change such as a new loan program (for example, going from a straight FHA to a 203K Renovation loan) a new addendum to the contract must be drawn up and signed by all parties.

Also included in this section is the financing contingency date, which identifies the date by which the buyer must receive loan approval from the bank. This has become an issue recently, as back in the old days, banks provided approval letters to both the buyers and sellers. In today's environment, loans are reviewed and re-reviewed due to fear of making a bad loan and having to repurchase a loan, thereby eliminating written guaranteed approval. There are too many moving parts so instead, lenders issue conditional approval, meaning there are conditions that must be satisfied by the buyer, title company or even sellers prior to closing. Knowing this, your job is to be sure you are given a minimum of 30 days—but preferably 45 days—from the signing of the contract by both parties. The date the contract is fully executed starts the loan approval clock.

There is another key section which states the buyer must apply for a mortgage on or before a certain date. This is critical for the case of a buyer who is not paying attention and allows this date to pass by. Failing to apply for financing within that period means an automatic default on the contract and forfeiting the deposit.

Section 9 is the last so-called critical section of the contract. This section identifies who pays what. This is the section where the seller may elect to pay or not pay certain closing costs.

As stated previously, because this section is based on a Florida contract, it would behoove you to ask your Realtor for a blank contract so you know where to look for any of these critical parts.

CONCLUSION

Now Go Buy a Home

Congratulations! You have now reviewed in detail the core points involved in obtaining a loan in today's new lending environment. I hope you've found the numerous exhibits, including the sample mortgage checklist, the do-it-yourself pre-qualification form, and the grid showing the new guidelines for those who have been involved in bankruptcy, foreclosure, or other situations, helpful. Unlike many publications (which require you to take a test), I believe the information contained in this book provides an adequate resource for any future homebuyer who is embarking on the process of obtaining a purchase or refinancing loan.

Should you wish to contact me, please feel free to visit my web page at www.joeadamaitis.com.

Good luck!